Whitewash

A Southern Journey through Music, Mayhem and Murder

ISBN 1-59113-187-1

Published by Frank Beacham

163 Amsterdam Avenue #361
New York, NY 10023

Cover photo by Bill Barley (© 1968, Bill Barley)

Booklocker.com, Inc.
2002

Whitewash

A Southern Journey through Music, Mayhem and Murder

Frank Beacham

To Carol…with love

Contents

Preface

What if you awoke one morning and, out of the blue, learned that many of the memories of your childhood were based upon an illusion? That the pleasant recollections about the quiet community where you spent the first eighteen years of your life were laced with carefully constructed myths. That your hometown was a facade—like a movie set—that masked terrible secrets, deep suffering, and unimaginable despair.

You also discovered that some of the adults that entertained you as a kid were not as kindly as you remember. Those cheerful, Ozzie Nelson-like businessmen that visited your parents' living room, you later learned, were often capable of extraordinary cruelty to the familiar, friendly people that you knew as neighbors in your own community.

Even the mere mention of your family name, you were told, brought instant dread to many local residents. For sixty years, that name had been associated with a horrendous abuse of power in a town divided by class and infused with fear. Under the tranquil surface, behind the inviting front porches, was a legacy of split families, quiet desperation, and defeated human spirits.

I grew up in the middle of it, yet it was all invisible.

The more I learned about the place I thought I knew, the more its veneer of normalcy disintegrated. What was once familiar began to take on new a dimension—a bit like revisiting an old puzzle I was unable to solve the first time. As long-held assumptions fell and the truth revealed itself, I questioned how I could have been so naive.

Slowly, I began to understand why my home state of South Carolina was such an enigma. I had lived there in a cocoon, an enclosed environment where a cultural artifice could be successfully constructed, sold, accepted, and maintained for generations. While in this protected cocoon, questions were discouraged. Doubt was ridiculed. Truth was denied.

There was only one way to transcend this contrivance. One had to break out of the cocoon, and then challenge it from the outside.

But I don't want to get ahead of myself. Many revelations about my life in the South came in degrees over time, as I became older and more experienced in the ways of human behavior. Other moments of awareness—the most powerful ones—came after I had reached my mid-forties and was living a decidedly non-Southern existence in Manhattan.

South Carolinians are deeply suspicious of natives who move to New York City. But, even as a teenager in high school, I always knew I would leave Honea Path, my hometown. It was a pleasant enough place, but there was little I wanted to do there. With fewer than 2,500 residents scattered throughout the town and surrounding rural community, it seemed that the only time people regularly assembled was at high school football games, Sunday church services and the annual Christmas parade. The town's social life, what little that existed, centered in a drugstore soda fountain on Main Street and at a drive-in burger joint about a mile away.

I avoided those scenes. They bored me. By the ninth grade, I had landed a dream job as a weekend disc jockey at WHPB, the local radio station seven miles north in the neighboring town of Belton. I was given awesome responsibility. Not only did I spin records, read commercials and take phone requests from my high school friends, I also "reported" the United Press International news on the hour, which I read with great authority. My most important function to station management, however, was the collection of cash from a bizarre stream of pay-as-you-go country/gospel singers and preachers who bought live airtime on the station each weekend.

Often, when broke, hung-over or just plain down and out, this odd assortment of misfit performers regaled me with stories of their adventures playing one-night gigs at dives throughout the South. More than once, impressed with a particularly creative hard luck story, I loaned a musician the money—about $12 as I remember—for a half hour of air time. I figured it was a good investment since I was getting the inside scoop on a world beyond the one I knew.

Not that my life in Honea Path was at all bad. I grew up in one of the town's best houses, the former home of the superintendent of the local textile mill. My mother was a popular high school history teacher. My father sold supplies to textile mills throughout the Southeast. We had a comfortable middle class home, and—because of my radio station job—I had more money in my pocket than I knew what to do with.

Yet, I yearned to leave Honea Path. When it came time to choose a college, I wanted to move three thousand miles away to attend film school at the University of Southern California. My mother was horrified. Yes, she wanted me to get a good education, but she insisted that I remain in the South. She pushed me to attend one of those small liberal arts colleges that dot the Carolina Piedmont. I knew exactly what she had in mind. She wanted me close by so her network of friends could keep a close eye on my activities. Not a chance, I resolved.

My father didn't care where I went to college. He was far more concerned that I turn out to be what he called "a company man." Be a Southern gentleman. Be loyal. Respect those in authority, he often said, and you'll rise through the ranks. He'd assure me: "If you're loyal to the company, the company will always be loyal to you." Upon hearing this fatherly advice and certain that my nature could allow me to be loyal to no company, I'd half-heartedly nod and make the quickest possible getaway.

On the college issue, I finally did a successful end run around my mother. I applied for and won a scholarship from the South Carolina Broadcaster's Association to attend journalism school at USC. Not the USC in California. The other one, the University of South Carolina in Columbia, about a two-hour drive from Honea Path. My proud mother was in turmoil about my leaving for what she called "the big city," but she couldn't refuse the scholarship. Finally, in the late summer of 1966, I escaped Honea Path.

The events of the next few years defined my life. I leaped out of the cocoon directly into the turmoil of the 1960s. Exploding like fireworks around me were the great issues of the times—the civil rights movement, the Vietnam War and the new freedom of the youth culture. I began to read Jack Kerouac and the Beats and discovered the powerful anthems of Bob Dylan. It was in this crucible that I decided to become a writer, and that I was first exposed to two of the stories that follow in this book.

As a freshman at the university, I worked at WCOS, a Top 40 radio station in Columbia. The program director, Woody Windham, introduced me to the sound of "beach music" and its companion dance, the shag. In the wee morning hours, I would play Woody's 45s from inside a filthy studio in a glass bubble atop Doug Broome's Drive-In, a local downtown hangout. Subsequent beer-soaked weekends in joints like the Beach Club and the Pad on the Carolina coast would complete the foundation for a lifelong love of rhythm and blues and all that's associated with it.

By my junior year, I had moved to a new job working on the night news desk at WIS-TV, the local NBC affiliate. The experience I acquired at WIS would, after college graduation, lead to a job for United Press International in Jackson, Mississippi. It was 1971, the tail end of the civil rights movement, a time when black candidate Charles Evers—brother of slain civil rights leader Medgar Evers—was running for governor and federal judges were busy issuing complex, book-thick school busing decisions. For a young reporter, Mississippi was a tough, no nonsense news training ground where you either wrote fast and accurately under pressure-cooker conditions or you didn't survive.

From UPI, I went to Gannett Newspapers, Post-Newsweek Television and the *Miami Herald*. After that I operated a television production company in Miami and Los Angeles. In 1991, to the amazement of my friends down South, I moved to New York City, a place Southerners seem unable to pronounce without dripping total disdain from each word. Now, after a decade in the city, I continue to pursue my work as a writer.

Once back east, I was able to visit South Carolina often. With the added perspective of urban life experiences, I came to better understand the South's remarkable myths, subtexts and contradictions. But it was a documentary film I saw in the mid-1990s, *The Uprising of '34*, that made me aware of my Southern legacy on a level much deeper than I had known before.

The film, and the remarkable series of events that followed its release, also confirmed my theory that it's important to first leave home (or the cocoon) in order to fully understand how home impacted your life. That space of time and place is the reason these stories are written from the perspective of an insider who, by happenstance, became an outsider. My outsider status, along with a natural skepticism and a professional reporter's understanding of the mechanics of the political cover-up, allowed me to pursue this material with some detachment.

That detachment, however, was not complete because there's a lot to like about the state of South Carolina. It's home to some of the friendliest, most outwardly hospitable people you'll ever meet. The native Southern cooking, when you're lucky enough to escape the fast food clutter to find it, is like nothing else in the United States. The music of the region, whether it be rhythm and blues, bluegrass, honky-tonk or gospel, thrives with each new generation of local artists. One can still hop in a car and travel the back roads of a picturesque rural landscape and discover unique people and places untouched by the compromises of urban life.

Along the way there are the old homes, flanked by huge, wraparound front porches shaded by the dense leaves of ancient oak trees. South Carolina is a place where people still lounge outside in wooden rocking chairs on a summer evening, sipping iced tea (always sweetened) and gossiping about the size and quality of the current crop of tomatoes in the neighbor's garden. It can be a warm, welcoming place.

But, as I learned so well, South Carolina can also be deceptive. Just beneath the surface of cordiality resides a resolute determination to protect and defend what are vaguely referred to as "Southern values." I wish I could precisely define what Southern values are, but I can't. Even for a born-and-bred native, nailing down the core beliefs that characterize white Southern culture is tricky business. That's partly because these values—if they are actually "values" at all—are ever-shifting and in a constant state of redefinition.

What's understood is that most modern Southern values revolve around issues of race, religion, property and money. When a value is deemed important by enough of the white Southern aristocracy at a given moment, it will be defended to the death (usually the death of whoever threatens the value).

It was only after living outside of South Carolina that I became sensitive to the linguistic sleight of hand that still infuses the speech of the region. Agendas and ideas are often camouflaged under a canopy of words and phrases worthy of a secret society. Breaking such code is an essential first step to understanding what makes the place tick.

For example, South Carolina newspaper obituaries of U.S. Rep. Floyd Spence, who died in office in the summer of 2001, repeatedly referred to the congressman, without explanation, as a "true patriot." The obituary of one of the subjects in this book described him as "a real Southern gentleman." What exactly do these phrases mean? I asked around, generating mild discomfort. One old-timer suggested the phrases signal that these were good old boys who stayed true to the values of the South and "didn't stray off the farm."

Another almost comical phrase is *so-called*. The NAACP's boycott of South Carolina tourism due to continued display of the Confederate flag was repeatedly referred to by white South Carolinians as the *so-called* boycott. Then, I heard the phrase again, and again. The *so-called* civil rights movement. The *so-called* Martin Luther King Jr. holiday. The *so-called* racial quotas. Finally, it hit me. *So-called* is a phrase used to preface a subject that white Southerners find offensive. *So-called* signals what's coming next has questionable legitimacy to the speaker. It's code, and Carolina speech is loaded with it. To understand the South, one must learn to decode its unique language.

Most explosive are the hot-button words that litter the Southern lexicon like land mines. Stumble onto one of these and you can find yourself in a heap of trouble. *Heritage* is one such word. Some white Southerners insist it's an innocent term used for describing the preservation of the area's customs and culture. But more often it's a euphemism to lament the fall of segregation in the old South. When Ku Klux Klan members talk of preserving the South's *heritage*, there's no misunderstanding what they mean. When *heritage* is evoked as a reason to fly the racially divisive Confederate flag on state property, the coded message is clear to those who still live by the Southern "values" of the Civil War era.

"There are always two issues in South Carolina politics: religion and race. Those who understand our politics really know this," Samuel J. Tenenbaum, a prominent Democrat, told me at a Columbia rally protesting the flying of the Confederate flag atop the state capitol. "South Carolina is fractured by race. The Confederate flag is a symbol of race. There will always be people in denial about this. But we're still fighting the Civil War, which is America's greatest tragedy."

One would not know this by studying South Carolina's recorded history. The carefully manicured historical works produced by local white historians would have us believe that it was the state's unique progressive qualities that allowed it to remain peaceful during the civil rights era. The high-profile violence that occurred in Mississippi and Alabama during the 1960s was mostly absent in South Carolina, the historians write with pride. Why? Because, as the white version of the story goes, South Carolina is a forward-looking state, a tolerant place where problems are solved with fairness and respect for all citizens, regardless of race or class.

From the black perspective, South Carolina remains a notoriously intolerant place. Rather than face its racial demons in the 1960s, South Carolinians collectively swept them under the rug—only to have them resurface thirty years later in a bizarre debate over *heritage* and an old flag that symbolized the state's segregationist past.

Whatever its origins, the contentious dispute over the state's official display of the Confederate flag succeeded in extending the Civil War into the third millennium in South Carolina. The flag was removed in 2000 from atop the statehouse dome only after the sustained application of economic pressure by the black community to the state's business interests. Rather than permanently banish this symbol of racism from public property, however, the legislature mandated—in what it termed a "compromise"—that the flag continue to fly in prominent public view from a thirty-foot flagpole at a busy intersection in front of the state capitol.

In late 2001, the flag debate erupted again when *heritage* advocates in the legislature attempted surreptitiously to substitute a lightweight nylon flag for the original, which was made of heavier cotton fabric. The reason: The colors of the cotton flag streaked when it rained, and the cotton cloth was too heavy to flap prominently enough except in the strongest of winds.

But it was early afternoon on April 17, 2002, in an astute piece of political theatre, that the flag drama reached a high point of absurdity. In full view of statehouse security, a protester identifying himself as the Rev. E. X. Slave, dressed in a black Santa Claus suit, propped a ladder against the flagpole, climbed it and set the Confederate flag on fire. Then he paused to autograph the pole. South Carolina's capitol security force tried to stop him with pepper spray, but, in classic Keystone cops mode, sprayed the chemical into the wind, sending it back into their own faces. To the cheers of onlookers, the blackened flag—burnt to a crisp— fell to the ground.

In 2002, the flag dispute continued to simmer. Any pretense that the issue was resolved in 2000 by removing it from the capitol dome was an illusion. The flag was simply relocated from one prominent location on public property to an even more prominent one nearby. Yet, the legislature's crude shell game temporarily cooled the heated drama, leaving the fractious squabble for another day. South Carolina's white leaders pretended the issue was behind them, though few black or white citizens were pleased with the outcome. An NAACP economic boycott of the state continued, black citizens who glimpsed the statehouse still got their daily reminder of the state's segregationist legacy, and the disgruntled white *heritage* advocates were more aggrieved than ever. In other words, it was business as usual.

So why couldn't South Carolina resolve the Confederate flag issue when it had a chance? The smart money said there was too much white Southern honor at stake. Removing the flag would have made it appear that the black community had won. That simply couldn't be allowed to happen.

One man who understood this was South Carolina state senator Robert Ford. During a November 21, 1999 television interview on *CBS Sunday Morning*, Ford, who is black, was asked about the NAACP economic boycott aimed at removing the Confederate flag from atop the state capitol building.

The legislator reminded flag opponents that they weren't going to resolve the issue with a barrel over the heads of the "white men" in the state. "These white men in South Carolina in 1861 started a civil war that lasted five years without a navy, army, air force or marine, because somebody was trying to tell them what to do. They're not going to buy into that (boycott). This is not Arizona. This is South Carolina—[home of] the meanest, toughest white men on the planet."

This book was born of my frustration with the grand illusions that are so skillfully used to deflect truth in South Carolina. The more that I tried to crack the surface of my subjects, the more I realized that much of the official history of my home state is essentially manufactured and was shaped to suit the prejudices and interests of the state's white ruling establishment. Stories of defining historical events—ones that did not fit comfortably with the self image of these power brokers—were discredited, ignored or, in one dramatic case, erased for more than sixty years through threats and intimidation.

The three stories in this book share much in common. Each vividly demonstrates how armed force, threats and violence were used to defend what white South Carolinians perceived at the time to be important values. Each resulted in human death, each led to intricate cover-ups designed to deflect the blame from those responsible, and each has been subject to censorship attempts by powerful interests. And, perhaps to no one's surprise, each continued unresolved well into the new millennium.

I suspect the reason for the lack of resolution is that each event shared elements of deep Southern cultural traits: stubbornness, pride, honor, and denial. With this heavy baggage, the long-term historical impact of each story remained in doubt. To date, not one of these events is described in detail in the state's history books.

Combined, these stories have given me a new understanding of where I came from and helped me begin to decode a Southern culture that has been so elusive for far too long. I invite you to join my journey and to make it yours as well.

Frank Beacham
New York City
August, 2002

Part One

Charlie's Place

Chapter 1 — Shaggin' the Night Away

Her stare was as cold as the draught beer she held in her hand. "Why," she angrily demanded, "do you have to bring the blacks into this?"

A few feet away, on the dance floor at Fat Harold's Beach Club, middle-aged white couples danced the "shag" to vintage rhythm and blues records. My interrogator at the bar was also white, in her late forties and a diehard shagger—part of the biannual migration to Ocean Drive to celebrate South Carolina's official state dance.

Her question surprised me. "Why would I *not* bring the blacks into the story?" I shot back. "This music and dance was invented by black people!"

The woman huffed, puffed and brusquely disappeared into the crowd, convinced I was some kind of troublemaker.

As I've found with so many cultural matters in my native South Carolina, it's much easier to skip along the surface and accept what one's told at face value. The most casual curiosity is often unwelcome. Asking too many questions can quickly turn disruptive, even with subjects as seemingly innocent as the state's native dance.

My unexpected adventure with what's known in the South as Carolina "beach music" began at a New Years Eve celebration in 1993 at a hotel in Greenville. Though I had devoured this regional strain of R&B in the 1960s at the University of South Carolina, my interest had faded in the years after I left the South.

On this festive night, however, the old memories came rushing back. Though the setting was a sterile hotel ballroom designed to host sedate corporate events in this booming Piedmont city, booze was flowing and inhibitions common to white Southerners were in temporary remission.

I watched meticulously dressed, middle-aged women from the upper crust of Greenville's white society cluster around the stage, gradually rising to a state of ecstasy through the hypnotic performance of a group of black musicians. Nearby, tuxedo-clad husbands watched with mild discomfort at the transformation of their spouses.

The music, a staple of the region for half a century, was loud and distorted—a sanitized R&B hybrid with simplistic lyrics celebrating youthful romance, alcohol highs and a carefree life at the Carolina beaches. The performance, by a popular group of Southern singers called the Tams, touched a deep chord with many of these women.

As the drink kicked in and male spouses were dragged into action, high heel shoes shot into the air and sweaty bodies gyrated across the dance floor. The Southern reserve that normally dominates this hardcore Bible belt community had taken a holiday. The evening quickly got down and dirty.

Though I had seen this spectacle many times before in my college days, the distance of time and detachment of place now made it more fascinating. The deeper meaning of this Southern ritual started to weigh on my mind.

As I watched the increasingly rowdy antics on the dance floor, it was clear that these black performers were piercing the carefully nurtured bubble of propriety so characteristic of upscale whites in South Carolina. Such passionate communal behavior is usually reserved for and tolerated at Southern sporting events. But as I listened to this familiar music from my youth, I was astonished to see these well-worn songs now generating a sexual tension in aging white adults.

The whole affair seemed so out of character for the place. Despite the seismic industrialization of the Carolina Piedmont in recent years, most of upstate South Carolina remained intensely conservative. The region has a history of right wing politics dating back to its Tory leanings during the American Revolution, and it was one of the first areas in the state to take to Republicanism after World War II.

The city of Greenville, in the foothills of the Great Smoky Mountains, is home to Bob Jones University, a fundamentalist Christian school that has long banned student dancing, drinking, smoking, kissing and hand-holding. Women wear ankle-length dresses on campus. Students caught attending a movie in town can be expelled. In March, 2000, only after being targeted with intense criticism during the state's presidential primary, did the school end a ban on interracial dating among its five thousand plus students.

Of Greenville County's 380,000 residents, more than seventy-seven percent are white, according the U.S. Census of 2000. This hub of conservatism is a place where the Civil War remains a hot-button topic and the ethics of slavery is still debated. It's also a place where mistrust between the races actively bubbles just beneath the surface of daily life.

Yet, it was clear from what I experienced in this Greenville ballroom that any racial divide ended on the dance floor. For a few hours, music and dance connected people who would have little or no connection the next day or the day after.

Questions began to explode into my mind. How did the "shag" originate? How did it become a popular dance embraced by white Southerners? Surely the dance and beach music—a derivative of R&B—must have roots in some kind of local black-white collaboration from another era. How could that interracial collaboration have occurred in the segregated South? How did blacks and whites get together to learn from each other? Was it done openly or was there some sort of secret alliance? Questions, questions and more questions.

Thus began a personal exploration, one that led me to a little known story that began in the Carolinas during the waning days of World War II. My journey took me through some uncharted territory, from popular white beach music hangouts like Fat Harold's and Ducks in the Ocean Drive section of North Myrtle Beach to a quiet black neighborhood a few miles south in Myrtle Beach. It was here that I discovered an extraordinary musical legacy that's been all but forgotten in the modern South.

Chapter 2 — Whispering Pines

The old saying goes that when Billie Holiday sang on the outdoor patio at Charlie's Place, the pine trees above—fanned by a gentle ocean breeze—whispered along with the music. To this day, that patch of trees on Carver Street is called Whispering Pines.

Whispering Pines is on "the Hill," a black neighborhood only a stone's throw from the noisy, neon-lit oceanfront pavilion and amusement park that now dominates the tourist district in Myrtle Beach.

Yet, as I drive down this modest street, with its scattered homes and businesses, there's little to reveal an illustrious past when hundreds of music lovers came to hear the likes of Louis Jordan, Billy Eckstein, Count Basie, Ray Charles, Duke Ellington, Lena Horne and virtually every significant "race music" artist of the 1940s and '50s.

Charlie's Place at Whispering Pines was run by Charlie Fitzgerald, a stylish black entrepreneur who, from the late 1930s until his death in 1955, operated nightclubs, a motel, a cab company, and—according to some—the beach resort's most notorious brothel.

I had been gradually introduced to the Fitzgerald legend in a series of informal interviews I'd done with dancers credited with inventing the shag. All were on the Carolina beaches in the years following World War II. I wanted them to tell me how the dance was created. As Harry Driver, George Lineberry, Betty Kirkpatrick, Chick Hedrick, Billy Jeffers and others independently told their stories, the name Charlie Fitzgerald repeatedly came up.

One by one the dancers each cited Fitzgerald as a significant cultural influence in the post World War II years. His name was always spoken with reverence, mystery and a sense of awe. It was if Charlie's old nightclub had been some kind of secret hideout that held the keys to a forbidden world. And each of these dancers, through good fortune, had gained admission.

There's no mention of Charlie Fitzgerald's name in South Carolina's modern history books. His contribution to his state's music and dance have been ignored, and today he's essentially a forgotten figure. To learn his story, an outsider needs to ask a fast-dwindling group of friends who still live and work in the old neighborhood, and a handful of music lovers—both black and white—who visited his club as teenagers.

One dancer suggested I talk with Dino Thompson, a beach music lover and lifelong restaurateur who had hung out at Charlie's Place as a kid. I found him at Cagney's Old Place, his restaurant on the Highway 17 tourist strip in Myrtle Beach.

"Charlie was one slick dude. He had an aura about him. He could have been the doorman at the Cotton Club," Thompson told me as he warmed to old memories. He had visited Charlie's Place as a youngster to hear musicians he could find nowhere else. "In 1952, Little Richard came to the Hill. He wasn't allowed to sing in the white clubs here. I begged my father to let the cook and two dishwashers in our restaurant take me. They sat me right up on the stage and I saw Little Richard in his blue suede shoes."

Dino Thompson wasn't the only Southern white kid who pined to hear black performers. In segregated South Carolina, where a prominent local radio station proudly advertised that it played "no jungle music," the provocative and sometimes raunchy mix of black gospel, jazz and blues was taboo. Labeled "race music," it was forbidden fruit that was rarely heard on mainstream Southern radio stations or sold in local record stores.

By 1950, however, the genie was beginning to come out of the bottle. A young *Billboard* magazine writer, Jerry Wexler (later to head Atlantic Records), published an article arguing that race music was more aptly called "rhythm and blues." The name stuck.

When WLAC, a 50,000 watt AM radio station in Nashville, switched to a black R&B format each night, it started reaching many white teenagers throughout the South. Disc jockeys Gene Nobles and John R became the first major links connecting black music to a white Southern audience. John R, a white South Carolinian and former actor, used his deep voice and a hepcat banter to convince many in the listening audience that he was a black man. (One of WLAC's savvy sponsors, Randy's Record Shop of Gallatin, Tennessee, sold the hard-to-find black music via mail order, delivering the disks to white customers in discreet, unmarked packages.)

Randy's modern day equivalent is Marion Carter, a white fan of black music who grew up to become one of South Carolina's top R&B record promoters. I spent half a day driving through remote countryside to his Repete Records operation in the tiny South Carolina town of Elliott. From a barn-like structure that seems more likely to house a small farming operation, Carter's employees ship hundreds of R&B recordings to music lovers and record stores each day.

"This was the devil's music—you just didn't listen to it in the average white Southern home," Carter told me. "White teenagers like myself were relegated to sneaking around to hear the music. We'd listen to WLAC at night out in the car or hide a portable radio under our pillow. What I have found as I've grown up and talked to people is there were tens of thousands of us all doing the very same thing in order to hear this music."

At the Myrtle Beach Pavilion, less than half a mile from Charlie's Place, white nightlife—as it was in other towns throughout America—was centered around the jitterbug, a strenuous, acrobatic dance usually performed to quick-tempo swing or jazz. The dance supported a subculture of fashionable young creative dancers known as "jitterbugs." The men were instantly recognized by their long blonde peroxided hair and custom-tailored draped peg pants, T-shirts, penny loafers and swirling gold chains. The women, favoring a simpler look, wore pedal pushers, angora sweaters and flowing scarves. These dance floor elites ruled beach society in the years following World War II.

By eight o'clock on most summer nights, hundreds of tourists gathered around the balconies and dance floor at the Pavilion. The star jitterbugs—known to the crowd by such names as Rubber Legs, Chicken, Bunk, the Roach and Little Robin—appeared one by one to show off their latest moves. Just as the streets in the Old West cleared when a known gunslinger appeared, the dance floor emptied for the kings and queens of the night.

One of the undisputed greats was Leon Williams, who was nicknamed Rubber Legs after he perfected a technique where he crossed his legs while standing and then began rocking from side to side, eventually sliding into a squat. "He was like a snake on the dance floor," an admirer proudly told me. "Nobody did it but Leon."

What few in the white Pavilion crowd realized was that Williams, along with a handful of other dancers on the beach, was adapting the jitterbug with tricks picked up from the black dancers in clubs like Charlie's Place. "The black dancers had a huge influence on us. They had rhythm and they interpreted the music," recalled Williams. "It still fascinates me how they felt the music so well."

Though Williams and his fellow dancers lived in a racially segregated community, they ignored the repeated warnings against associating with blacks that came from South Carolina's political and social establishment. "The colored girls danced with white boys and the colored boys danced with white girls," said Williams. "We hugged each other's neck. If you had been at the beach in that period of time you'd thought segregation didn't exist."

The white dancers' fascination with black music and culture extended beyond the nightclubs. "We used to go to colored churches on Sunday because we loved the gospel music," said Williams. "We wanted to hear our friends clap their hands and sing. They really got into it and that impressed me. We realized early on that you can dance to gospel music."

Partially due to the passion of another talented young dancer, George Lineberry, R&B was finding its way onto the jukeboxes in the white dance halls and pavilions along on the Carolina coast. Big George, as he was nicknamed, installed records on the coin-operated machines for a local amusements company. He took it upon himself to move the most popular records from the jukeboxes in the black clubs, including Charlie's Place, to the white dance halls.

Big George, who died in 1999, was an immensely popular fixture at the beach and was often slipped a few bucks by concerned parents to dance with a daughter who needed a boost in self-esteem. With great ceremony, he made it a point to "test" each new record installation with a personal spin on the dance floor. In South Carolina, the R&B that could be heard only at the beach joints became known as "beach music."

In the 1940s, the young dancers found the beaches a liberating place. For many it was the first time in their lives that they were in a community where no one knew them or their family. "There was a special freedom in that," disc jockey John Hook mused one night as he spun records at a crowded beach dance club. "That meant they could let it hang loose and do stuff they'd never dare do at home."

This precious anonymity, Hook shouted over the club's roaring decibel level, also gave the young white men and women a chance to escape the pressures of a segregated society and to emulate what they liked best about their contemporaries in the black community. "There was a certain sensuality, a certain sexuality that put it all out on the edge," he said.

"The guys knew when they went out on the dance floor that a hundred women were watching them right at that moment and that each would give anything to be their partner. Man, that's some heady, heady power. Imagine the confidence that produces in you. Imagine what happens to your body when you know—you absolutely know for sure—that you're gonna score tonight."

The best of the young male dancers, said Hook, concentrated on their female partner. "The great dancers never danced to the crowd. They gave their whole attention to the woman. They fired on her with great subtlety, sophistication and eloquence. It was not a dance about doing steps, but a dance of moving with her. It was a mating dance. It didn't always lead to sex, but it led to intimacy."

Chapter 3 — The War Years

It was in the summer of 1945—the waning days of World War II—that the lure of black music began to take hold among white dancers. Until that time, artists like Stan Kenton, Gene Krupa, Tommy Dorsey, Lionel Hampton and Glenn Miller drove a dance culture based on big band swing and jazz. However, an unlikely convergence of events on the Carolina coast was to broaden the Southern dance repertoire.

One sprang from the logistics of war. Though most of the beach dancers were too young or, for one reason or another had received deferments from military service, the war still had a huge impact on their daily lives. An inconvenience that would later prove to have a significant effect on the dance was the government-imposed banning of bright lights along the coastline.

"You couldn't have lights on the beach at night because they could be seen by enemy submarines off the coast," explained Harry Driver, one of the top beach dancers, in a conversation before his death in 1998. "All the windows and the top half of car headlights had to be painted black until the summer of 1945. If they blew a siren, it was a warning that a submarine was off the coast and all lights had to be turned off."

The lighting restrictions temporarily drove beach nightlife 125 miles inland to the resort area of White Lake, North Carolina. It was here, at hangouts such as the Crystal Club and the Hayloff, that the dancers met a continuing stream of soldiers preparing for war at nearby Fort Bragg and Camp Lejune.

"During the war years our dance styles were influenced at White Lake," said Driver. "Soldiers came to that area from all over the world. I met great dancers from Chicago, New York and California. It was at White Lake that I learned from those soldiers a lot of the steps that have long been attributed to me. It was a real melting pot of dance."

But the same war that brought the regional dancers together was also decimating the big bands that produced their favorite music. Depleted of musicians gone to combat and hindered by increasingly high costs, large traveling orchestras virtually disappeared in the war years, replaced by small combos of six to eight musicians. The musical experience was not the same.

"When big bands went out of vogue, there were many more black musicians left to perform in their place. I think that opening for the black performers had a lot to do with the crossover of black music to white audiences," said Chick Hedrick, a beach dancer who later operated the popular Chick Hedrick's Domino nightclub in Atlanta.

That black music was essentially banned in the segregated Carolinas didn't hurt either, added Driver. "They called it 'suggestive music.' You've got to understand," he said, "when we were growing up, 'Sixty Minute Man' implied that you could last sixty minutes doing the big trick. A white Southern society was not going to listen to that. The music was parental repulsive. Lyrics like 'Sock it to me, baby, one more time' or 'I'm gonna smoke you all night long' made the parents go crazy and left the teenagers wanting to hear more. Plus it had the tempo we liked to dance to."

Chicken Hicks, a charismatic beach legend who emerged from another dance hot spot, Carolina Beach, North Carolina, noted a clear distinction between the raw beach music of the 1950s and the sanitized "bubblegum beach" that emerged as a popular Southern party music during the 1960s.

"The new crap from bands like the Embers is not beach music. It's college bop. The [original] beach music was race music," said Hicks. "Bull Moose Jackson had a song called 'Bow Legged Woman Just Fine.' 'Old legs built like barrels/wide in the middle/jump start/slamming the straddle.' You didn't hear that kind of stuff on white jukeboxes."

Most of the top white dancers agree that it was a mix of jazz, blues and gospel music that fueled the transition of the jitterbug to the popular slower, smoother dance that's known in the South today as the "shag."

Spanning the popularity of both the jitterbug and the shag was Bill Pinkney, an original member of the Drifters and a 1988 inductee into the Rock and Roll Hall of Fame. "The only thing that separates the shag from swing and the jitterbug is the movement, the rhythm of the body and the footwork," said Pinkney, sitting at his kitchen table in Sumter, South Carolina. "I can shag at my age (then seventy six), believe it or not."

Though there's continuing disagreement over the exact origins of South Carolina's state dance, those who created it gave major credit to the black dancers of the era, many of whom did an erotic dance that mimicked the act of copulation known as the "dirty shag." In fact, the very definition of the word *shag*, according to the *Oxford Dictionary of Modern Slang*, is "to have sex with." It appears, however, that the slang term did not come into common use in America until years after the dance became popular in the Carolinas.

"I first heard the term *shag* at Charlie's Place," said Big George Lineberry, who left the beach in 1948. "They called it the shag on the Hill. I think the shag and dirty shag came out of Charlie's nightclub."

Henry "Pork Chop" Hemingway, who eventually became the first black policeman in Myrtle Beach, was a close friend of Charlie Fitzgerald and the official chaplain at the club during its heyday. He now runs a taxi company on Carver Street, a few steps away from where the club once stood. Hemingway watched the dance evolve over many years and emphasizes there is a clear difference between the dirty shag and the dance now called the shag.

"The dirty shag was basically a bump and grind type of thing," Hemingway said. "The shag was altogether different. It was a smooth dance. The first person I ever saw do it was a girl from Elloree, South

Carolina. She did it so well they nicknamed her 'Shag.' That's where the word came from. It was a girl's name."

That girl, Cynthia Harrol, waited tables and worked behind the bar at Charlie's Place, said her aunt, Dora Lee Goings. Possessed of a friendly, outgoing personality, Harrol lived to dance. She made repeated trips to New York City, where she tore up the dance floors of Harlem's top nightclubs. Everyone, Goings said, wanted to dance with Shag.

The modern version of the shag probably was born in the black clubs, agreed Dino Thompson. "The jitterbug is just an offshoot of the lindy hop. When you throw in some really acrobatic stuff and some flamboyant moves from the lindy hop to the triple-time swing, you've got the jitterbug. The blacks took it to another level with their creativeness and flexibility. The shag is the jitterbug on Quaaludes...the jitterbug slowed down."

Harry Driver, an early member of the Shag Hall of Fame, said "the jitterbug was done by a bunch of footloose, fancy-free zoot-suiters—both black and white—from Chicago, New York and all over the South. "I recall seeing a lot of the dancers who would bring the girl in, swing her over their shoulders and never miss a beat."

However, the jitterbug took on a different meaning for Driver in 1946 when he saw two dancers come together and then do a very smooth, full 360-degree pivotal rotation on the dance floor. "It set me on fire because I saw so much more to the dance than acrobatics." Driver would later perfect the pivot, earning a reputation for his smooth, effortless execution on the dance floor.

Black dancers, said Driver, brought a rhythm that was largely missing with white dancers. "It was the beat—the way they moved. They had a history of African tribal dance. What we learned from the blacks was their rhythm and tempo—the moves. You watch a white person do a syncopated walk and then watch a black do it. The blacks put more into it than you can imagine. We emulated what they did. Everybody claims to have started the shag. Nobody started it. It evolved from one dance to another in a big melting pot."

Charlie Fitzgerald stirred that melting pot. "When I came to Charlie's club he'd say 'Little Dancin' Harry, come on in, man! You ain't gotta pay!' Charlie was as nice to me as any white guy has ever been on any beach I've ever worked on," Driver remembered. "I loved the guy because he loved me and we both loved dancing."

Love of dance and a welcome atmosphere is also what brought Betty Kirkpatrick, a Shag Hall of Fame dancer from Carolina Beach, to Charlie's club. "It was the music and dance that drove us. It had nothing to do with color."

George Lineberry had warm memories of his nights at the Hill—many ending at daylight. "Charlie once told me, 'George, you got a little black in you.' I knew the black music had a better beat. It would turn me on a little more. I was the best at the belly roll and the dirty shag. I could lay it on them."

For young Dino Thompson, the belly roll—or "vertical sex" as it was also called—was the ultimate shag step, a move that had been perfected by dancers at Charlie's Place. In his personal memoir, *Greek Boy*, Thompson offers a description of the belly roll: "Boy pulls girl close enough to touch belly buttons. Then, in rhythm, they throw one leg out together, then the other. Slick and sexy."

The belly roll and a 10-cent song on the jukebox, recalled Thompson, was "your license for romance. Pick out the girl of your dreams, lead her out to the dance floor, ease her out of a fast sweaty pivot into a tight belly roll and bruise your excited private parts all up against hers. Then, right as the lyrics get down and dirty, burn her down with your Tyrone Power eyes."

As I gathered bits and pieces of Charlie's story from those who knew him in his old neighborhood, it became evident that his unique take-charge persona served to elevate his image within the community. Not only did Charlie Fitzgerald's nightclub patrons see him as exceptionally stylish, but he was a man who commanded their respect.

Chick Hedrick, who would later own and operate his own nightclub, remembered being impressed with how well Charlie managed his place. "He wore a pistol on his side. Nobody bothered anybody there. He didn't need that gun to keep the peace, though. He wore the gun because he was the boss. He was the law there and everybody knew it."

In fact, it was Fitzgerald's aura of control and gangster style that's still most remembered in his old neighborhood. At night, he often wore striped suits, round-collared white shirts, kitty bow ties, suspenders and Stacy Adams lace-up boots. Sometimes he'd wear hats, usually a round Stetson derby or an Al Capone-style fedora. By day, he'd put on denim overalls with his white shirts. "Not just overalls, but starched, clean overalls. The man was a cat…sharp, slick," recalled Leroy Brunson, who grew up in the Whispering Pines neighborhood and now lives directly across the street from the vacant grove of trees that was once Charlie's Place.

Under those clothes, however, everyone knew that Fitzgerald packed weapons. "He carried a .45 and a .38 all the time. He had holsters that ran around his shoulders," said Brunson. "Charlie was a man of few words. He didn't talk much. But when he told you something, he meant what he said." Then Brunson paused, as if to reconsider his hardball take on Fitzgerald. "Charlie was a bluffer, though. He'd scare a lot of people by pulling a gun out and firing it into the floor or in the air. He'd do this during fights or if he wanted somebody to leave and they didn't want to go."

As a rebellious teenager, Henry Hemingway learned the hard way that Charlie was boss. "Back in those days, I loved to fight. I'd go up to Charlie's Place at night and turn the place out...just raise hell. He'd say 'Boy, you got to quit this! You got to quit this!' One night I went there and stepped on a guy's foot, and he asked 'What did you step on my foot for?' I hit him."

Hemingway said he'll never forget what happened next. "Charlie put his nickel-plated shotgun in my mouth and said, 'Son, hell has overtook you.' I was scared outta my mind and that was the last big fight I ever had."

When he was a little older and wiser, Hemingway experienced another side of Fitzgerald. After spending several years playing trumpet in his college band, Hemingway returned home to Myrtle Beach unable to afford his own horn. "Charlie bought me a trumpet. 'Here boy,' he said, 'maybe you'll make something out of yourself.' He would do things like that for kids. He was a good man."

Chapter 4 — South Carolina, circa 1950

During the years following the war, the white beach dancers forged their own unique counterculture along the Carolina coast. Some supported themselves as lifeguards, bingo callers or dishwashers, while others proudly lived off the continuing flow of young female tourists who visited the beach in the summer.

"You've heard of tennis bums? I was a dance bum," Chicken Hicks told me over breakfast in an Ocean Drive coffee shop. "I'd get a little money off the girls. I didn't work much. The girls liked to dance with the beach crowd. I'd put the poor mouth on. Tell them I was a little bit down. I'd get names, and hell—in the wintertime—I'd travel around to these different towns (to visit the girls at home). I just didn't work. I was sorry as hell."

Jo-Jo Putnam, another Shag Hall of Fame dancer and sometime professional pool player, recalled a beach lifestyle in the 1940s and '50s that he claims put Jack Kerouac and the Beat Generation to shame. "We were hip, we were first and we were real. While the Beats drove a car across the country, we stole the car. We laughed at those phony motherfuckers. We encompassed all walks of life, from bank presidents to bank robbers."

Putnam apparently felt the need to prove to me, even though he was over sixty, that his survival skills were undiminished. Just outside a packed Columbia dance hall, he abruptly stopped our interview, jumped out of his chair, and ran behind me. Within seconds, he was wielding his long switchblade knife firmly against my neck. From that point on, I left his assertions unchallenged.

It wasn't so much the dancers' carefree ways that bothered the powers that be in South Carolina, but their disregard for the state's social rule that the races shouldn't mix. Even in Myrtle Beach, a frontier town always more forgiving in matters of sin than the rest of the state, the jitterbugs constantly flirted with the edge of the law.

"There were always policemen looking to lock somebody up on the beach," remembered Driver. The charge might be dirty dancing, having too much to drink or swearing in front of an officer of the law. "I got arrested one night for saying 'No damn kidding, I better get a beer before they close.' The cop reached over and grabbed me and said 'You're going to jail.' I said, 'For what?' He said for using loud and profane language in a place of business. I said all I said was 'damn.' He said 'You're still going to jail, kid.' But before he could book me they had taken up a collection at the Pavilion for my bail. This happened to everybody from time to time. All they wanted was a fine. They only wanted the money."

Money, everyone knew, was the mother's milk of law enforcement in the beach community. Charlie Fitzgerald, as a successful black entrepreneur operating in a segregated town controlled by whites, followed the rule that to survive he had to pay for protection. "I saw Charlie with a cigarette carton—one of those tall boxes that cigarette packs come in— jammed full of money, nothing but bills to go to some law enforcer," said Hemingway. "I can't prove anything today, but law enforcement got mighty rich back in those days."

Even if the eyes of the law looked the other way from his various business enterprises, Fitzgerald's coziness with whites was out of sync with the time and place. Racial tension in South Carolina began escalating after a federal judge opened the state's Democratic primary to black voters in 1948. It was to the chagrin of many Southern whites that blacks began to assume a few positions of power.

"To the surprise of a great many 'traditional' Southerners, there is a Negro alderman in Winston-Salem, North Carolina. Richmond, Virginia has a Negro city councilman and a Negro state representative," reported Bem Price of the Associated Press in June, 1950. "Even here [Columbia, South Carolina], headquarters for the States Rights Democrats, a Negro undertaker was in the race for city council. Another is running for the council in Chattanooga. Two reportedly may enter the race in Nashville."

The political awakening of the South's black citizens was at the core of the racially charged 1950 Democratic U.S. Senate campaign in South Carolina. The incumbent senator, Olin D. Johnston, entered the summer campaign bolstered by the successful attempt by Southern state senators to block the establishment of a permanent Fair Employment Practices Commission (FEPC), a federal agency that would investigate racial discrimination in employment practices.

In bombastic Southern oratory, the earthy Johnston—his arms flailing wildly—railed in a speech on the floor of the U.S. Senate that it would be "a blow to Christianity" to require equal treatment of whites and blacks in hiring. "A responsibility has been placed on mankind to keep his race pure," argued Johnston. "Mongrelization of the races is the greatest destroyer of civilization and Christianity."

In his deep baritone voice, Johnston decried "persistent agitation, designed to cause all colored people to have such a group consciousness as to carry continuously a chip on their shoulders," and warned his fellow senators "not to mine the road ahead with dynamite that is certain to explode with great destruction when these opposite viewpoints collide."

Back home in South Carolina, anxious to exploit the race issue to the maximum in his campaign for reelection, Johnston stumped the state's forty-six counties in a series of verbal slugging matches with his opponent, incumbent governor Strom Thurmond. It turned into quite a show. In the towns along the campaign trail, the political rallies leading up to the July 11 Democratic primary were considered top-flight summer entertainment. Boisterous crowds of up to four thousand turned out for the carnival-like stump speeches, demanding that the candidates mix it up with an exchange of barbs and insults. For the first time, newly empowered black voters joined the mostly white crowds. It didn't matter to either candidate that the rising black constituency would witness the most openly racist political campaign in the state's modern history.

The two candidates worked hard to outdo each other with caustic race-baiting rhetoric. Thurmond accused Johnston of being soft on racial segregation and promised if elected to the Senate that he "will not sit with folded arms and my tongue cleaved to the roof of my mouth" when a federal court makes a civil rights ruling that attacks the southern way of life.

"Any man that says I am for mixing of the races is a low-down, contemptible liar," charged Johnston in a speech at Georgetown. In another appearance at Charleston, the senator—loudly booed by blacks in the crowd—shouted to his hosts, "Make those niggers quit!"

Johnston, who darkened his graying hair with black shoe polish, sometimes found moist black streaks running down his forehead in the humid evenings of summer. Thurmond, a health fanatic, became well known for standing on his head on the lawn of the governor's mansion.

At two stops a day in the grueling campaign, the candidates hammered each other on race. Thurmond was accused by Johnston of inviting the governor of the Virgin Islands, a black man, to the South Carolina governor's mansion. Thurmond was irate. "No Negro will ever be a guest at the governor's mansion so long as I am governor," Thurmond shouted to a chorus of boos from blacks at a rally in Columbia.

At a rally in Spartanburg, Thurmond chided Johnston for his tenure on the Senate's District of Columbia Committee. "If he's got so much influence, why does he let the Negroes swim in the same pools with white people?" Thurmond barked.

When they weren't berating each other on race, the candidates were using paid political ads to polarize South Carolina's electorate. In a newspaper ad for his candidacy, Thurmond urged President Truman to forget about "minority blocs" of voters and withdraw his program to break down segregation in the armed forces. He warned that Truman's desegregation plan would "compel Southern white boys to serve, eat, and sleep together with Negro troops and also use the same recreational facilities."

The governor even published an attack on Paul Robeson, the celebrated black singer and actor. Robeson, Thurmond charged, "has been going all over the country demanding that we abolish segregation, and to show his contempt for our way of life in the South, he married his son off to a white girl."

Robeson, one of the most talented and politically active black performers of his time, had toured the South in 1948 on behalf of progressive presidential candidate Henry Wallace. Thurmond, presidential candidate of the segregationist Dixiecrat party that year, represented everything Robeson abhorred.

Robeson was a black man Thurmond couldn't intimidate, and the popular singer knew how to get under the governor's skin. Risking life and limb to sing his way through the South, Robeson attacked the Thurmond-led Dixiecrats as "powerful reactionaries who hope to stamp out the militant struggle of the Negro for complete freedom, equality and civil rights [and who] hope to keep all the wealth for themselves."

Framing the "black belt of the South" as the area that would decide whether the Negro people "survive or perish," Robeson spoke with a level of public candor then uncommon in South Carolina. "For as long as any boy or girl can be denied opportunity in Alabama, Georgia, South Carolina and Mississippi—so long as one can be lynched as he or she goes to vote—so long as the precious land does not belong to the people of that area (and with the land, the wealth that flows there from in agriculture and in industry)—so long as they do not have the full opportunity to develop and enrich their cultural heritage and their lives— so long are the whole Negro people not free."

To the South's white establishment, those were fighting words.

Chapter 5 — The Ku Klux Klan Attacks

As racial passions flared in the Senate campaign during the summer of 1950, the Ku Klux Klan, whose local members had kept a low profile for many years in Myrtle Beach and surrounding Horry County, sprang back to life. Led by Grand Dragon Thomas L. Hamilton, a Leesville grocer, Klan members in South Carolina were emboldened by the racially explosive political climate.

At a July rally attended by two thousand people in Wagner, South Carolina, Hamilton railed on about a wide assortment of the Klan's enemies, a grab bag that included blacks, Jews, Catholics, communists, congress, newspapers, radio and the United Nations. He prayed in public and sought the help of God in the Klan's crusade against evil. It was about this time that Klan members took it upon themselves to punish those citizens in the community they considered moral deviants.

Beatings and cross burnings became rampant in North and South Carolina. Unmarried couples were awakened in the night and flogged with buggy whips. A cross was carved into the head of a pregnant black woman. Dozens of men and women were severely beaten and left naked miles from their homes.

By midsummer, the Klan turned its attention to Charlie Fitzgerald. To them Fitzgerald was a black man breaking all the rules. He was wealthy, successful and fearless. "He went where a lot of black people couldn't go," recalled Brunson. "When we went down to the Cozy Corner to order a hot dog, we'd have to stay outside. When Charlie wanted something, he'd just walk right in the door and sit down. When Charlie went to the movies he went right to where the whites sat. He didn't go upstairs with the blacks."

The reason he got away with it, Brunson mused, is that Fitzgerald defied all the stereotypes that whites had of blacks at the time. "He was a real light-skinned man. People looked at him differently because he was dressed nice, he always drove a brand new convertible car, and he'd wear those hats."

With the escalated racial tension of 1950, however, Fitzgerald's luck ran out. In an intimidating visit to his nightclub, Klan members demanded that white patrons no longer be admitted. "They told Charlie they didn't want the white kids there listening to music," said Hemingway. "Charlie told them to go to hell. They warned him they were coming back."

It was a warning that Fitzgerald kept to himself. "He had his gun ready, but few others knew about it," said Hemingway. "If Charlie had told the general public about the threat, there would have been a bloodbath. 'Cause everybody would have tried to help him."

At 9 p.m. on Saturday, August 26, the Klan staged a motorcade through the streets of Myrtle Beach. Scores of nightriders, outfitted in white KKK regalia, cruised the town in more than two dozen convertibles. The lead car had a fiery cross made up of glowing red electric light bulbs mounted on its left fender. Local police provided traffic control.

"All of a sudden everything got quiet...an eerie quiet," recalled Harry Driver, who was at the Myrtle Beach Pavilion at the time. "We turned around to see what was happening and we saw all these convertibles coming down Ocean Boulevard. They had on white sheets and cone hats. I get cold chills right now just thinking about it."

Betty Kirkpatrick, the white dancer, watched the caravan—announced by loud blaring sirens—from nearby Highway 17. "It was the most frightening thing I have ever seen," she said. "It's not pleasant to talk about."

The Klan motorcade snaked slowly through the black neighborhoods of Myrtle Beach. Eventually it reached Carver Street, the automobile-lined roadway used by club-goers for parking during visits to Charlie's Place. As the intimidating convoy passed his crowded establishment, Fitzgerald became enraged. He picked up the phone and called the Myrtle Beach

Police Department, warning that if the Klan returned, there would be bloodshed.

Instead of providing the club with protection, police passed Fitzgerald's message directly to Klan members, who took it as a dare. "Ladies and gentlemen, we being white Americans could not ignore that dare from a Negro," Hamilton, an organizer of the parade, recalled later at a Klan gathering.

Just before midnight, about sixty Klansmen in twenty-five vehicles—this time with sirens silenced—made a return trip to Charlie's Place. Fifty-nine-year-old Charlie Fitzgerald waited defiantly for the white-sheeted mob outside the club. He was six feet, three inches tall, 190 pounds, balding, with a thin mustache. In each hand he gripped a pearl-handled pistol.

The arrival of the nightriders was swift and violent. A furious rush of ghost-like men streamed from the cars, immediately striking Fitzgerald in the face and seizing his weapons. Overwhelmed, he was thrown into the trunk of a Klansman's car. There, locked in darkness, he listened helplessly as windows were smashed, tables and chairs overturned, and a volley of more than five hundred rounds of ammunition was sprayed into the wooden building that held his friends and customers.

"People were screaming, hollering, running everywhere. And the police were nowhere to be seen," said Brunson, who witnessed the attack as an eight-year-old boy.

Suddenly, in the midst of the fury, the music stopped. The club's jukebox—the most powerful symbol of the cultural fusion that had united young blacks and whites in the postwar years—skipped, sputtered, and went silent as it was riddled by a hail of bullets.

"From the way some Negroes left with window panes around their necks and in a hurry, it would seem something was going on inside," Hamilton said sarcastically, as he described the attack to Klan supporters a few weeks later at a public rally.

After wrecking the club, the Klan members—with Charlie Fitzgerald still locked in the trunk of a car—quickly left the scene.

Gene Nichols, who operated another nightclub on the Hill, was shot in the foot. Clubgoer Charlie Vance sustained internal injuries from a beating he received at the hands of several Klansmen. Cynthia Harrol, the dancer nicknamed Shag, suffered an injured back after being beaten. Klan members then crushed her fingers by slamming shut the cash register drawer as she tried to secure the club's money.

A Klansman, left behind by his cohorts, lay bleeding on the ground. A bystander drove him to a local hospital. When doctors lifted his blood-soaked sheet, it was revealed that the man was wearing a police uniform. James D. Johnston, age forty-two, an off-duty police officer from neighboring Conway, died within an hour from a .38 caliber bullet wound. The coroner said he was shot in the back. His assailant was unknown.

As Johnston lay dying, his fellow Klan members viciously whipped and beat Fitzgerald on a deserted road near a local sawmill. A Klansman used his knife to slice off a piece of each of Fitzgerald's ears. Bleeding and nearly senseless, Charlie Fitzgerald was left on the road to die.

It was not to be. A defiant Fitzgerald pulled himself up and staggered slowly to Highway 17, the main inland business thoroughfare along the Carolina coast. There he was picked up by a motorist and taken back to his nightclub.

At 3 a.m., Sheriff C. Ernest Sasser drove to the nightclub and arrested Fitzgerald. Rather than take him to a local hospital for medical treatment, Sasser quickly transported Fitzgerald to an undisclosed jail three hours away in Columbia. The sheriff then took a public stance of silence, revealing no information about the arrest—including what Fitzgerald had been charged with and why he was taken so far away from Myrtle Beach. Newspapers speculated Fitzgerald was taken to the prison hospital at the state penitentiary.vHowever, no public records exist that even document that Fitzgerald was arrested at all.

The attack on Charlie's Place shocked both white and black Myrtle Beach residents, many of whom were surprised by the viciousness of the Klan's actions. For a significant number of local blacks, it was cause to leave town.

"The aftermath of the terrorizing visit of the Klan to the Hill was the loss of colored employees by hotels and guest houses here at the beach," reported the *Myrtle Beach Sun*. "Many colored waitresses and maids, fearful of a return visit of the Klan, left town Sunday and Monday and this week a number of hotel operators have reported they were without domestic help of any kind."

After publicly denouncing the violence at the nightclub, Myrtle Beach Mayor J. N. Ramsey offered a tepid explanation for what triggered the attack. "Some of the conditions that probably caused the Klan to parade through this particular area of Myrtle Beach, namely white people patronizing colored business establishments or visiting in colored sections for amusement purposes, are not approved by the Southern people generally, but they are absolutely legal," the mayor said in a written statement after the shooting.

Five days later, Sheriff Sasser made a live radio address that was carried by stations in Myrtle Beach and Conway. In it he cleared Charlie Fitzgerald, who was still in jail, of committing any crime related to the attack and said he found no evidence that any Negro had fired a gun in the fracas.

Sasser, as had other law enforcement officers, speculated that James Johnston, the Conway policeman, was shot in the back and killed by a fellow Klan member. In his radio address, the sheriff placed full blame on Klansmen "who left him on the ground to die." Earlier, the Associated

Press quoted an unidentified state law enforcement official who contended Johnston was shot and killed "in a bout with robed and masked men." No one speculated as to why the Klan would kill its own man.

The sheriff denied a widespread rumor that Charlie's Place had been attacked because Fitzgerald "was keeping a white woman for immoral purposes." He did suggest, however, that the young white dancers who frequented the nightclub had influenced the Klan's actions. "To my knowledge some white men and women do go to this place on special occasions to hear the orchestra and watch the colored people dance," the sheriff said. "I have on many occasions told them it was not a good policy."

The sheriff ended his address by attempting to convey the extremist nature of the Klan's activities while acknowledging that the organization still had strong community support. Sasser told listeners that the Myrtle Beach radio station on which he spoke had been warned that if it carried any information about the Klan it would be blown up. But then he quickly added: "I happen to know a few men that are members. Some are from good families. They were led into this unfortunate thing with no intention of committing a crime."

Just before Sasser went on the air, his department began arresting a handful of Klan members for the attack on Fitzgerald's nightclub. Grand Dragon Hamilton was the first—picked up as he was driving alone to the nearby town of Florence. He was quickly released on $5,000 bond.

As the night wore on, others were arrested. R. L. Sims Jr., a beer truck driver, was rustled from his bed in the middle of the night. Dr. A. J. Gore, a Conway optician; Clyde Creel, a service station operator; and June Cartrette, a farmer, joined the list. By the following day, ten Klansmen were under arrest and lawmen said they were looking for one hundred more, though that number was never apprehended. All those arrested were charged with conspiracy to incite mob violence.

Meanwhile, Charlie Fitzgerald—charged with no crime—remained in an unknown jail.

Why? Perhaps to protect him from attack by Klan members working in law enforcement, speculated Henry Hemingway with a quiet chuckle. "You see, Sasser and Charlie were actually good friends. The general feeling was that Charlie was making a lot of money for Sasser. But there were certain things with Sasser being white that he couldn't do or say. On the inside, though, he would help Charlie."

About two weeks after the attack, Fitzgerald was released from jail under a $300 bond as a material witness and promptly arrested again during a taxi ride in Columbia. The charge was possession of a weapon and an obscene motion picture. He was fined $76 and released.

In a rare interview after the proceeding in city recorder's court, Fitzgerald told a reporter he had been holding an automatic pistol on the seat next to him for protection. "I know it was against the law to have that gun, but it was right in my conscience because my life has been threatened and I am still in danger." The film, Fitzgerald added, was collateral for a three-dollar loan he had made to a friend who was short of cash.

The club owner confirmed he had been held in three jails since the attack, but wouldn't say where. His mood was conciliatory, and he said he had been treated well while in custody. He praised Sasser, saying "I've never known a straighter white man in my life."

In a parting comment, though, Fitzgerald displayed the street smarts that had made him a survivor. "I'm a free man—and I'm not a free man," he declared. "I don't know who is or who isn't a member of Klan."

Chapter 6 — The Aftermath

After the Klan arrests, Grand Dragon Hamilton began campaigning for public sympathy. "When a Negro fires at a Klansman, we will fire back," he said. "Whenever a Negro tells me to stay away, there'll be trouble." The Klan leader also vigorously denied that Officer Johnston had been killed by a Klan member at the shootout.

The emboldened Klan organization in the Carolinas broke with tradition and did not mask their faces in parades and demonstrations. "The traditional Klan robe includes the hood that covers the face, but no member of this organization whatsoever covers his face," Hamilton said. The reason, he explained, is that the Carolina area Klan members are "white gentlemen" who are neither afraid nor ashamed to be recognized in their regalia.

Hamilton's boast came from a genuine confidence that the Ku Klux Klan enjoyed significant support in the white beach community. After all, Klan rhetoric had carefully targeted the moral sensibilities of the region's conservative Baptist churchgoers. Race was a red-hot political issue, and President Truman's attempts to bring racial reforms to government and private institutions had been unpopular throughout the South. It was perhaps no coincidence that just after the sheriff had made his well-publicized Klan arrests, the Broadway Theater in downtown Myrtle Beach offered the movie *Masked Raiders* to its patrons.

On October 5, the Horry County grand jury supported the sentiments of many the area's white residents. Even with substantial proof of their involvement, five Klan members, including Hamilton, were cleared of all charges relating to the attack on Charlie Fitzgerald and his nightclub. The white grand jurors refused to indict the men on charges of conspiracy to commit mob violence. A strong plea to the grand jurors by Judge E. H. Henderson that "no group or organization, by whatever name or style, has the right to set at naught the laws of our state" fell on deaf ears.

All other Klansmen charged in the case had been released after an earlier preliminary hearing found no probable cause for their arrest warrants. A coroner's jury ruled that unknown persons caused Officer Johnston's death. His murder was never solved.

Two of the beach community's local newspapers, the *Myrtle Beach News* and the *Horry Herald*, had little to say about the release of the Klan members. Neither felt it significant enough to report the grand jury's action on their front page.

Within weeks of the shooting, the U.S. attorney general directed the FBI to investigate the Klan attack. However, M. W. McFarlin, special agent in charge of the FBI's Savannah, Georgia office at the time, permanently stonewalled the press, refusing to discuss what he called "the Fitzgerald case." There is no evidence an investigation ever took place.

In November, a feisty Hamilton—wearing a bright green cloak—spoke from the back of a truck to a crowd of eight thousand gathered at a Klan rally in a tobacco field near Myrtle Beach. Backed by a twenty-foot-high flaming cross and flanked by a handful of men and women wearing red Klan uniforms, the Grand Dragon retaliated against Sheriff Sasser for his arrest.

"I have affidavits showing that some people are having to pay law enforcement officers for the privilege of doing business," Hamilton bellowed to the crowd. On his lectern, an American flag was draped over a Bible. At his feet, more than a hundred white-sheeted men stood guard, acting as a buffer from the assembled masses.

To the Klan's accusations of graft, Sasser responded to the press after the rally: "Enemies stop at nothing; they say I accept graft. Well, I have one thousand dollars to give to anyone who can prove from reliable information that I ever took a dishonest dollar."

The proof never came, but it didn't matter. Sasser's arrests of Klan members eventually cost him his job. In 1952, the Klan flexed its political muscle and worked to defeat the sheriff in his bid for re-election. The loss was overwhelming, with Sasser carrying only four precincts in the entire county. One of those he did carry was the "Race Path" precinct that included the Hill area of Myrtle Beach. The precinct's black residents voted 343 to 6 for Sasser's re-election.

The man who beat the sheriff, John T. Henry, was sympathetic to the Klan and accused of being a member. Although his Klan connection was never proven, Henry's police force was later charged with violating the civil rights of blacks.

Olin D. Johnston was re-elected to the United States Senate in 1950, beating Strom Thurmond for the Democratic nomination in the primary. He served until his death in 1965. Thurmond got another chance to run for a Senate seat and was elected as a write-in candidate in 1954. He holds the record as the longest-serving member of the Senate.

"No one can say with certainty that the recent political campaign in South Carolina contributed to the outbreak of violence there," wrote John Lofton of the attack on Charlie's Place in the September 5, 1950 issue of the *Arkansas Gazette*. "But it was obvious that both candidates in the United States senatorial contest were inflaming racial antagonism."

Charlie Fitzgerald eventually recovered from his injuries and returned to his nightclub. Some whites still came to hear the music, but many were now afraid to visit the Hill. The days of innocence were over. "I never went back there after that because I knew it would not be safe," Harry Driver lamented. "They would hate me because I was white, even though I had nothing to do with it."

Young Dino Thompson is one who did return, making the mistake one night of allowing Fitzgerald to catch him staring at his now legendary ears, whose healed scars were faintly visible. "I thought the Klan had put Ks in his ears and I would kinda peek at them," remembered Thompson. "Charlie saw me staring and said 'you trying to look at my ears, boy.' I said 'no sir, no sir.'"

Hemingway said that after the Klan attack Fitzgerald was "basically the same guy, but a little meaner."

What Hemingway and others also remember is that while all the Klan members went free, Fitzgerald ended up going back to jail, even though I could find no court records or press clippings to document it or explain why. "Charlie went back to jail in less than ninety days for something related to the shooting," Hemingway said. Though he doesn't remember the charge, Hemingway estimated Fitzgerald remained in jail for a year or more. This was confirmed by Leroy Brunson; his brother, Henry; and Elijah "Kidnapper" Goings, all close friends of Fitzgerald at the time.

"They put Charlie in prison," said Leroy Brunson. "They were trying to blame him for shooting the Klansman even though they never found any evidence." A now-deceased Hill resident, said Brunson, was beaten by police and threatened with drowning in an attempt to get him to implicate Fitzgerald in the killing. The man refused.

"More or less, they wanted to get Charlie out of the way," said Hemingway of the white establishment that ran South Carolina at the time. "If they had left him alone, Charlie would have been one of the first real rich black men ever to come out of Myrtle Beach."

The lack of records documenting Fitzgerald's return to jail doesn't surprise Hemingway, who in 1955 joined the police force as Myrtle Beach's first black officer. "Back then, black people had no voice whatsoever. None. You'd be surprised how many things would come down from the state to a little place like Myrtle Beach in those days. After thirty-two years that I have as a policeman, I've seen so many crooked things in law enforcement it makes me puke."

Hemingway remained Charlie's friend until the club owner's death from cancer on July 4, 1955. "It was the only time I ever saw him break down—he was in his bed sick—and I started praying for him," said Hemingway. "I remember part of the prayer was 'God, if it's your will that Charlie must leave us, prepare his soul. We are not worried about how long he stays here, but where he goes hereafter.' At that point, Charlie broke down. He died a little after that."

Though Charlie Fitzgerald's contributions are virtually unknown to the thousands of white shaggers who keep the dance alive more than a half century later, the influence of his club—and the crossover of black music to a white audience—are repeatedly cited by the pioneers credited with inventing South Carolina's state dance.

"Black music influenced us from the start, and the only good place to hear it was on the Hill," said Billy Jeffers, a popular jitterbug—and Shag Hall of Fame member—who began working at the Carolina beaches in the summer of 1938. "We learned to smooth it out and do more with just a little bit of music. Being there made you think you were at the best place in the world."

Added Harry Driver: "We had integration twenty-five years before Martin Luther King [Jr.] came on the scene. We were totally integrated because the blacks and whites had nothing in our minds that made us think we were different. We loved music, we loved dancing, and that was the common bond between us."

Chapter 7 — Fast-Forward a Half Century

In late September, 1998, the beachside streets of Ocean Drive in North Myrtle Beach are packed with more than twelve thousand middle-aged white shaggers as they barhop between dance clubs such as Fat Harold's, Ducks, Pirate's Cove, the Barrel, the Spanish Galleon, the Boulevard Grill and the Ocean Drive Pavilion. This ten-day festival of shag is the annual Fall Migration of the Society of Stranders (SOS). (A similar annual spring festival is called the Spring Safari.)

Shagging is big business in Ocean Drive, a small resort community about twenty miles north of where Charlie Fitzgerald's club once stood. On Main Street, Judy's House of Oldies sells hard-to-find beach music records and instructional shag videos, while Beach Memories caters to coastal nostalgia with lithographs, clothing, coffee mugs and bric-a-brac that commemorate legendary South Carolina beach hangouts like The Pad and Roberts Pavilion.

The best of the white beach dancers are memorialized in a Hollywood-style Walk of Fame along Ocean Drive's sidewalks. Storefront windows display a mountain of shagging kitsch, from T-shirts, cheap watches, and beer bottle covers to specialty ship cruises organized for shag dancers.

Though the music played by the elite group of disc jockeys in these thriving beach clubs is still mostly R&B, there's rarely a black face to be found among the affluent group of mostly fifty-something couples who keep the shag alive. On the Carolina coast, the unique biracial collaboration that created the dance a half century ago has all but disappeared. These days the aging white dancers find their beach excursions—with all the boozing and social camaraderie—a pipeline to their youth and a release from the pressures of the modern world.

"For many people this is an outlet. It's like a drug. They get high on the music—the energy of the show," said General Johnson, a veteran black singer-songwriter whose group, Chairman of the Board, has long been a staple of the Carolina beach music scene.

Another enduring beach music act on the Southern club circuit is Maurice Williams and the Zodiacs, whose recording of "Stay" has long been a beach classic. "Shaggers want the nitty-gritty real thing," said Williams, who is black, noting that he grew up with his white audience, most of whom are now in their forties and fifties.

"The beginning of beach music was predominantly rhythm and blues," said Williams, "but today if you say to a young black man, 'come on, let's go and listen to a beach music show,' he'll say 'I ain't going to that white music.' The average black kid in his twenties or thirties doesn't know what this is all about. They see a beach music festival and think it's all white music. It's strange. They haven't studied the history of their music and the guys who recorded it enough to know what beach music is all about. They just don't know any better."

Leroy Brunson, still an avid dancer in his mid-fifties, avoids the white shagging scene at nearby Ocean Drive. "I watch the shaggers now on TV and sometimes I have to laugh," he said. "They are doing this shag and beach music now, but we invented it. They just kind of took it away. They just claimed it."

If the blacks lost part of their culture, Southern whites gained something precious from their brief creative fling with race music and dirty dancing in the 1940s and '50s. "Beach music and shagging was a celebration of life that was new for Caucasians," said John Hook. "It was an emulation of what white people thought they were seeing in the black community. Beach music isn't the music or the dance or the attitude, it's all of those married together and what it has become over time. Lots of people listen to this music today and don't know why they like it. They just know that something was missing in their life."

The staff at Charlie's Place, early 1950s.

Charlie Fitzgerald, Sept. 1954

Cynthia "Shag" Harrol, early 1950s

(Photos by Jack Thompson)

Leon "Rubber Legs" Williams, early 1940s.

Harry Driver, 1957

(Photo by Jack Thompson)

Big George Lineberry
(left) & Harry Driver, 1994

(Photo by Frank Beacham)

Part Two

The Legacy of
the Orangeburg Massacre

Chapter 8 — The New South Turns Old South

It was early in 1968, my junior year at USC, when I began getting my journalistic feet wet in a job working on the night news desk at WIS-TV, the NBC affiliate in Columbia. I did everything—from reporting, to writing scripts to shooting and processing the reels of black and white 16mm news film. Working alone, I'd quickly comb my hair, turn on the camera and run around in front to perform the on-air "stand-upper." I was, in local TV parlance, a "one-man band."

Over several nights in early February, I used a newsroom receiver to monitor police radio communications concerning an escalating series of disturbances in the nearby town of Orangeburg. A transmission during the night of February 8 brought news that in the latest clash some black students from South Carolina State College had been killed and many more were wounded. From the radio account, it sounded as if the students had fired weapons at a group of highway patrolmen, and that the patrolmen, all white, had returned fire in self-defense. One message came through the radio static loud and clear: blame for the deaths was clearly being placed on the students and what the police called "outside agitators."

At nineteen and still a very novice reporter, I had yet to learn to think and act independently within the crucible of Southern culture in which I swam. My awareness of the shooting, like most of those around me at the time, was filtered through the prejudiced accounts of South Carolina's local political establishment and the ultraconservative print and broadcast media that supported it. Yet even from the earliest official explanations of what happened in Orangeburg, there was skepticism. It took a leap of faith to believe the state's story, but most white Southerners did just that. For me, the seed of doubt existed from day one, but it remained dormant for twenty years.

Once I began to seriously focus on the event, I came to understand its larger meaning and the startling fact that no resolution had come. What apparently began as a racially inspired shooting quickly evolved into a complex cover-up by senior officials of the state of South Carolina. At first, the cover-up worked. Later, it unraveled. As the thirty-fifth anniversary of the shooting approached, the story of the Orangeburg massacre continued to simmer unresolved in a twilight zone of blame and denial.

The tragedy at Orangeburg has remained one of the least known and most misunderstood events of the civil rights era. On a basic level, Orangeburg is a chilling history lesson on the horrors of law enforcement motivated by racism and hatred. Over time, it evolved into a remarkable character study of white leadership in what was once proudly hailed as the "New South." As a window to Southern culture, the saga of the massacre is drenched in themes and values that have motivated South Carolinians since the Civil War.

It all began when an act of racism in a small college town led to peaceful protest by frustrated black students. The governor, elected on a platform of racial moderation, responded with a vast show of armed force. Each side misread the other, escalating the conflict. Then, in a peak of emotional frenzy, nine white highway patrolmen opened fire on the students. In less than ten seconds, the campus became the scene of a bloodbath.

This scenario played out over four days. On the final day, three students were killed and twenty-seven others wounded when the lawmen sprayed buckshot—the deadly oversize shotgun pellets used to hunt big game— onto the campus. Most of the students, in retreat at the time, were shot from the rear—some in the back, others in the soles of their feet. None carried weapons.

The killings occurred in a Southern state heralded for its record of nonviolence during the civil rights era. In an attempt to preserve a carefully cultivated image of racial harmony, a web of official deceptions was created to distort the facts and conceal the truth about what happened in Orangeburg. The state claimed the deaths were the result of a two-way gun battle between students and lawmen. The highway patrolmen insisted their shooting was done in self-defense—to protect themselves from an attacking mob of students. To bolster that claim and deflect responsibility from its own actions, the state hastily devised a media campaign to blame the riot on Cleveland Sellers, a young black activist working to organize area college students.

To date, the public official who was ultimately responsible for the student deaths has failed to explain the series of events that spiraled out of control during his watch in the winter of 1968. As he nears the age of eighty, it appears that former governor Robert McNair—a proud and stubborn man of Scotch-Irish ancestry—is still in denial over his actions during the student protests and could ultimately take the secrets of Orangeburg to his grave.

For the promising young leader who was lauded for his progressive views on racial issues, the future was not supposed to turn out that way. South Carolina had become a different place during the eighteen years following the Ku Klux Klan attack on Charlie Fitzgerald's nightclub. Despite a determined struggle against civil rights reform, rapid change was bombarding the old aristocratic social order. Racial barriers were finally falling.

Although its elected officials had done all they could to resist the court-ordered desegregation of public institutions during the 1950s and '60s, South Carolina had ultimately lost the battle to remain a segregated society. Public support for the Ku Klux Klan dwindled. The harsh race-baiting politics of Strom Thurmond and Olin D. Johnston in the 1950 Senate campaign were largely abandoned in favor of more moderate themes that included improved education and economic development.

Thurmond, the fiery old segregationist, radically changed his racial colors over the years to become a political survivor. Unlike his contemporary, Governor George Wallace of Alabama, who repented for his racial sins before his death, Thurmond offered no apologies and flatly denied in later years he'd ever engaged in racist politics at any time during his career.

A new era of Southern politics was well underway in 1965 when forty-four-year-old Lieutenant Governor Robert McNair ascended to the governorship after the incumbent, Donald Russell, resigned to appoint himself to the U. S. Senate seat left vacant by the death of Olin D. Johnston. McNair, a small-town lawyer and former legislative leader from the Hell Hole Swamp section of Berkeley County, came to office with a reputation as a congenial consensus builder.

Born December 14, 1923, South Carolina's future governor grew up on his family's farm in one of the poorest areas of the state's low country. Most of McNair's neighbors were black, though very few minority residents were registered to vote and none held positions of power in the community. McNair liked to say that because he grew up with black people, he knew all about them and their needs.

Yet, as the son of a white farmer and merchant in the heartland of the state's white ruling-class aristocracy, McNair was raised in a time of complete segregation of the races. As a young man he learned that good manners and the preservation of outward appearances are vitally important to proper Southern society. Polite South Carolinians cared for their Negro neighbors—helping them during times of sickness and trouble. The knee-jerk racism that plagued Mississippi and Alabama was not present in South Carolina. Yes, the races might be segregated here, but it was the duty of the privileged white ruling class to be the caretakers of their black neighbors—that is, as long as those neighbors remained in their place.

To those weary of the old fire-breathing racial demagogues, the youthful McNair's non-threatening, accommodating style was a genuine breath of fresh air. After making it clear that he would embrace and expand the racially moderate policies of Ernest F. Hollings and Donald Russell, the governors who preceded him, McNair was quickly labeled by the media a progressive leader of the "New South." In no time, he became one of the most visible new faces in the national Democratic Party.

Upon taking office, McNair promised the state legislature that he would "communicate, cooperate, and coordinate" with members. He called a joint meeting of the heads of all state agencies and ordered them to put aside interagency rivalries and begin working together. He courted black voters and maintained good relations with the leaders of the state's NAACP. His openness and accessibility earned rave reviews in the early days of his administration.

The state's national reputation was important to the new governor. To maintain his progressive image, McNair wanted none of the racial strife that had engulfed Mississippi and Alabama during the civil rights protests of the era. In fact, he made it a point of great pride that South Carolina had avoided the wrenching street violence familiar in a growing number of states. Civil disturbances were bad form and would never be tolerated in South Carolina, McNair insisted.

As a young member of the state legislature during the 1950s, McNair— like his white colleagues—had little interest in advocating equality for black citizens. He gained a reputation as a progressive not because he was an activist, but because he wasn't a rabid segregationist in a state full of them. McNair's pragmatic side saw that the South was eventually going to lose the battle to maintain segregation. For a politician barely thirty years old, it was best to look ahead and define the issues important to the future of the South. By the time he'd achieved the governorship, McNair had defined his mission: to push South Carolina from its rural past to an industrial future. He would do it by accelerating economic growth. Racial stability—along with an improved educational system— were important lures that would attract outside business interests to the state, he reasoned.

McNair's political focus on economic growth was in direct collision with the political currents of the times. Protests against the Vietnam War and race riots in major Northern cities were tearing down the most durable governmental facades. The appearances of social stability that McNair so valued were rapidly evaporating in the nationwide cultural upheaval. The accommodating young governor, who had assumed the top office two years earlier, also began to change.

In his 1967 inaugural address, McNair offered a hint of this change and a clue to his uncharacteristic actions a year later during the tense days of hostility in Orangeburg. As Alabama governor George Wallace and his wife, Lurleen, looked on from the speaker's platform, McNair said, "I intend to use all the authority and influence at my command to see that the good name of our state is not tarnished."

The New South's conciliator was turning into an old South law and order hardliner.

Chapter 9 — "Governor, I'm Afraid Something Terrible Has Happened"

The massacre at Orangeburg might have been an obscure footnote in South Carolina history had it not been for the efforts of two young journalists who were skeptical of McNair's public statements in the days following the shooting. While the rest of the nation's press accepted the spin that the killings were the result of a two-way gun battle instigated by "outside black power advocates" against the police, Jack Bass of the *Charlotte Observer* and Jack Nelson of the *Los Angeles Times* slowly chipped away at South Carolina's official version of events.

I was introduced to Jack Bass under unusual circumstances. It was the summer of 1968, a few months after the Orangeburg killings, and we were among a handful of reporters waiting in Robert McNair's suite at the Palmer House in Chicago for the governor to receive an important phone call. Outside, in the streets, all hell was breaking loose in a police riot. Demonstrators repeatedly chanted "the whole world is watching" as the 1968 Democratic National Convention was transformed into a globally televised antiwar protest.

Inside, when the expected call finally came, Governor McNair was informed that it was Sen. Edmund Muskie of Maine, not he, that Sen. Hubert Humphrey had chosen as his vice presidential running mate. McNair, who had been publicly touted as a front runner for the vice presidential nomination, took the news with grace, as always. But, as we would soon learn, it was the beginning of the end for what had been a charmed political career. The killings at Orangeburg had already taken a toll on the young governor.

Two years later, Bass and Nelson would publish a groundbreaking book of investigative journalism that documented how McNair and his administration had covered-up the state's role in the killing of the college students. Titled *The Orangeburg Massacre*, the book depicts the events in exacting detail and has become the definitive factual account of what actually happened in the days before and after the shooting.

The setting of the tragedy was South Carolina State College (now University), one of two small black colleges located in Orangeburg, a mostly white, ultra-conservative community of 20,000 located about forty miles southeast of Columbia. Although South Carolina State and nearby Claflin University—with a combined enrollment of about 2,300 students—insured a substantial well-educated black population in the town, a social wall divided the races. In 1968 white Orangeburg was a hotbed of segregationist radicalism—a center for organizations resisting the social change sweeping the South. The South Carolina State campus, made up of students from mostly poor and middle class black families, was a cultural world apart from the white neighborhoods surrounding it.

Though there was an undercurrent of tension among black students over the second-class treatment their school was receiving from the state, the seeds of conflict that led to the Orangeburg massacre began at a bowling alley. John Stroman, a black South Carolina State senior from Savannah, Georgia, had a passion for bowling. All Star Bowling Lanes, the only bowling facility within forty miles of the campus, refused to admit black patrons. Its owner, Harry Floyd, believed that the presence of black bowlers would hurt his business. His stubborn refusal to serve black customers—including students from the local colleges—elevated the bowling establishment to a highly visible symbol of the remaining segregation in Orangeburg. A group of students, organized by Stroman, decided to stage a protest.

On Monday, February 5, 1968, Stroman led the student activists from his campus to All Star Bowling Lanes. About forty young protesters entered the facility before Harry Floyd was able to bolt the door. "Some of the fellas went to the counter," Stroman recalled. "Every time they touched something, like a napkin holder, the whites would throw it in the trash. When we put money in the jukebox to play a record, [Floyd] unplugged it and gave us our money back."

When the students refused to leave, Floyd called the police and asked to have them arrested for trespassing. Orangeburg police chief Roger Poston, convinced that the situation was explosive, ordered the bowling alley closed for the night. The students returned peaceably to campus, vowing to return.

Harry Floyd was able to deny service to black citizens because of a legal ambiguity in the 1964 Civil Rights Act. Though the legislation contained a section on public accommodations, it covered only businesses engaged in interstate commerce. It was not yet clear whether the law applied to bowling alleys. A complaint targeting Floyd's refusal to serve blacks had reached the Justice Department for a determination of whether the U.S. government should take the issue to federal court. At the time of Stroman's demonstration, however, the government had not yet decided to pursue the case, leaving Floyd temporarily free to operate a segregated establishment.

The following night Stroman and his fellow students returned to All Star Bowling Lanes for a second protest. This time, however, they found the doors to the bowling establishment locked shut. Instead of encountering Harry Floyd, the young protesters were met by a group of heavily armed law enforcement officers, some carrying three-foot-long wooden riot batons.

The centerpiece in this menacing show of force was South Carolina's top law enforcement officer, J. P. "Pete" Strom, a heavy-set, rough-edged authoritarian often compared to legendary FBI director J. Edgar Hoover, both for his bulldog appearance and autocratic reputation as "Mr. Law Enforcement." Usually dressed in ill-fitting, baggy suits and displaying a crossed-pistols tie clasp, Strom was prone to skip the niceties and carry out his own brand of old South law enforcement. Although the state's white leaders praised him for showing restraint in some civil rights demonstrations, many blacks viewed Strom as a dangerous and arbitrary symbol of white police power. Young whites, especially those protesting the war in Vietnam, shared an equal disdain for Strom.

Strom's staunchly conservative bias was visible during a protest over the controversial awarding of an honorary degree to General William C. Westmoreland by the University of South Carolina on June 3, 1967, just eight months prior to the Orangeburg killings. Then commander of American troops in Vietnam, Westmoreland was a highly divisive figure in a volatile time. After a group of peaceful antiwar protesters were threatened by pro-Westmoreland supporters at the campus ceremony, Strom summarily ordered that the protesters—not Westmoreland's supporters—be removed by police from the area where the general was to receive his degree. Asked why he moved against the peaceful antiwar activists rather than those who had caused the trouble, Strom indicated that Governor McNair wanted no antiwar demonstrations to mar the ceremony honoring the general.

McNair, the fourth governor to re-appoint the politically powerful Strom to the position of top cop, dispatched him to Orangeburg to confront the students challenging Harry Floyd's segregation policy. McNair and Strom were cut from the same cloth, and the governor placed his complete trust in the veteran lawman. Unfortunately for the students at Orangeburg, when it came to protest, the patience of both men had worn razor thin. By 1968 McNair and Strom had been hardened by television images of race riots that began at Watts in Los Angeles and moved to Boston, San Francisco, Newark, and Detroit. In a news interview preceding Orangeburg, McNair commented that officials in Detroit had "waited too late to call in force" to squelch the riots that left forty-three dead and caused $50 million in property damage. Riots would not be allowed to occur in South Carolina, the governor insisted.

Upon their return to All Star Bowling Lanes, the students got a low-key reception from Strom and Orangeburg police chief Poston. The two officers calmly explained to Stroman that under the current law Floyd had the right to file trespass charges against his group if they entered the bowling alley. If that happened, those inside would be arrested.

That understood, the doors were unlocked, giving the students the option to enter. About thirty black men and women then walked through the door. They quietly waited a few minutes before Floyd asked them to leave. At that point, Strom suggested to Stroman there was no need that everyone in his group be arrested; he could make his case just as strongly in court with no more than one arrest. Responding to the suggestion, Stroman told the female students to leave and advised others to exit the premises if they did not want to be arrested. Fifteen students remained.

The arrests did not sit well with the gathering crowd outside in the parking lot. Jeering and shouting escalated into anger. Another student was arrested for cursing at a policeman. As word of the arrests reached campus, several hundred additional students headed to the bowling alley. Along the way, some picked up loose bricks and scraps of wood from a demolished building.

Fearful of a violent confrontation, Strom and Poston did an about-face and decided against holding the fifteen students that had been arrested. Each was immediately released from the town jail into the custody of South Carolina State's dean with an understanding that they return to the parking lot and attempt to convince their angry classmates to go back to the campus.

Just as Stroman and the others moved to calm the crowd, however, the Orangeburg police made a serious mistake. Chief Poston, who had been in Orangeburg only three years, had—as a precaution—ordered a fire truck sent to the shopping center. What Poston failed to realize was that a previous generation of black students had been sprayed with fire hoses on a cold night during a sit-in demonstration in Orangeburg in 1960. The fire truck had become a unique symbol of police oppression to blacks in the Southern town. Upon spotting the red truck, the mood of the crowd took an angry swing. The night was bitter cold and the students thought the high-pressure water hose was about to be turned on them.

As most of the crowd moved toward the fire truck, a few students tried to enter the bowling alley. When police responded, a student was pushed into a glass window, causing it to shatter. Within moments, all hell broke loose. Police, joined by highway patrolmen, started wildly swinging their wooden clubs at the protesters. Several coeds were viciously knocked to the ground by the lawmen. A female student, held by two policemen, was brutally beaten by a third. As John Stroman tried to help a fellow student being struck by two patrolmen, he was sprayed in the face with a chemical and thrown off his feet by a blow to his stomach. As the police violence escalated in the parking lot, white bowlers—oblivious to the chaos outside—calmly continued their play without interruption.

Bloodied students, helped by classmates, straggled into the college infirmary. Others, infuriated by the police assault, threw bricks and rocks at white-owned businesses in Orangeburg as they returned to campus. Forty miles away at the state capitol, Robert McNair sat stunned in the governor's office as Pete Strom reported a vicious attack on the police by the students.

A year earlier, the hands-on governor would probably have traveled to Orangeburg to address the problem in person. A visit by the governor to the bowling alley might have intimidated owner Harry Floyd enough to change his mind. At the very least, it would have demonstrated to the students that the state's chief executive was on their side in ending Floyd's last ditch effort to preserve segregation. This time, however, McNair resisted personal negotiation. Instead, he upped the state's show of force by sending 250 National Guardsmen and additional highway patrolmen to Orangeburg. It would be the biggest mistake of his political career.

By the morning of Wednesday, February 7, the conflict had moved beyond a simple protest over a segregated bowling alley to the issue of police brutality. The unwarranted beating of black college students by an all-white police force was being misrepresented by law enforcement officials as a riot caused entirely by the students. Matters were made worse by Orangeburg's insensitive white city officials, who refused to grant the students a parade permit and responded unconvincingly to their grievances. The government's only response was force and more force. As hundreds of armed white men moved into Orangeburg, the area's segregationist congressman, Albert Watson, added another log to the growing fire.

"What is occurring in Orangeburg at this moment is just another step in an overall plan to disrupt this entire nation," Watson said in a statement to the news media. "Hearings before the House Committee on Un-American Activities, on which I serve as a member, have proved without a shadow of a doubt that these riots are planned long in advance by the so-called civil rights leaders and groups which are bent on destroying the democratic process."

Watson commended law enforcement officials in Orangeburg for their "magnificent efforts in putting down this threat of anarchy." They acted "swiftly, positively and courageously in putting down this riot. Certainly the entire nation can look to the example set by these gentlemen in Orangeburg, South Carolina, and gain insight into the proper way to curb a serious civil disturbance."

Within hours of the beatings, a highly publicized blame game began over who was responsible for blemishing the state's spotless public image for racial peace and stability. An "outside agitator" stirred up the students, Governor McNair and law enforcement officials told the media in an effort to portray the police beatings as a reaction to a violent riot instigated by the students.

The alleged culprit was Cleveland Sellers, age twenty-two, a bright, driven young native of the town of Denmark, located only twenty miles from Orangeburg. Sellers was not a typical black South Carolinian. He had been a Freedom Fighter in the 1964 Mississippi Summer Project to register African American voters. As a dedicated teenage activist, he was introduced to Mississippi through a frightening, high-profile assignment to help investigate the disappearance of civil rights workers James Chaney, Andrew Goodman and Michael Schwerner. Under the cover of darkness, Sellers, with a partner, had risked his life to unsuccessfully search the backwoods, swamps, and hillsides of Philadelphia, Mississippi for his murdered co-workers.

Having quickly matured into an effective civil rights organizer, Sellers became national program director of the influential Student Nonviolent Coordinating Committee (SNCC). The organization's advocacy of black self-awareness and pride—labeled the "black power" movement by the national news media in the 1960s—put fear in the hearts of many white South Carolinians who believed they were the target of some sort of terrorist organization. Sellers, with his hip goatee and voluminous Afro, became the perfect embodiment of their fear.

The truth is Cleveland Sellers had no interest in John Stroman's bowling alley protest. He had declined Stroman's invitation to participate and was out of town the first night the students visited All Star Bowling Lanes. He showed up the second night only after the arrests had drawn a crowd. Sellers, who was also a vocal opponent of the Vietnam War, had come to Orangeburg to promote a campus organization, the Black Awareness Coordinating Committee (BACC). But the exact nature of his current mission didn't matter to the white community—reputation alone kept Cleveland Sellers under constant surveillance while in South Carolina. It also didn't matter that he was only a casual observer of the bowling alley protest. Sellers' very presence was enough for Pete Strom and his men to identify their scapegoat.

Daybreak, Thursday, February 8, came after an uneasy night of scattered protests. Because Orangeburg was "very tense and dangerous," South Carolina State's acting president, Maceo Nance, urged students to remain on campus. "We again impress upon you that your personal safety is in jeopardy," Nance said. In Columbia, Governor McNair again escalated the forces in Orangeburg. He also appealed to the White House to pressure the Justice Department to take legal action against Harry Floyd for his refusal to admit black patrons at the bowling alley. New requests for the governor to visit with the students in Orangeburg were refused.

As the day progressed, Orangeburg was transformed into an occupied town. Not since Sherman's march had the city seen such a concentration of armed might. Rumors swept the white community that black militants planned to burn the city to the ground. The National Guard was ordered to protect utilities from attack. Governor McNair told the press, "We want to avoid property damage and injury to anybody."

Thursday afternoon, the commander of the state highway patrol, Col. Frank Thompson, told his men to use firearms only as a last resort if their lives were in danger. That decision, he implied, was left to each individual patrolman. Thompson then returned to Columbia for the night.

As dusk turned into a near-freezing darkness, a paralyzing tension seized the town. Rumors of apocalyptic proportions spread from neighbor to neighbor. Frightened store owners, skeptical of any unknown customer, kept loaded shotguns at reach under their counters. The silent night was periodically jarred as false fire alarms sent sirens screaming throughout the streets. As the evening wore on, there were isolated disturbances, each of which ended as quickly as it began.

At the Claflin Campus, a group of students hurled rocks and other objects toward policemen. There were police reports of sporadic sniper fire on or near the Claflin campus and an attempt to burn down a warehouse used by law enforcement. When a reporter heard a loud explosion, he was told that a patrolman had fired a shotgun into the air as a warning. Even with the students from both colleges off the streets and secure on their respective campuses, the white community remained on pins and needles—waiting for some anticipated cataclysm.

With the quiet grounds of South Carolina State surrounded by ranks of armed white men, Henry Smith, an eighteen-year-old sophomore committed to civil rights causes, led a restless group of fellow students to a block-long side street at the southwest corner of the campus. There, at about 9:30 p.m., they built a bonfire using wood and scraps picked up from a nearby construction site. The mood of the students—giddy and gleeful—was in sharp contrast to the grim lawmen standing nearby. As the fire blazed, the flames eventually drew a crowd of about two-hundred from the nearby dorms. Warming themselves by the roaring flames, the young people sang traditional civil rights songs, including "We Shall

Overcome" and "We Shall Not Be Moved." For the students, it was a spontaneous release from an extremely tense day. It was also a small act of defiance to show they would not be intimidated by the absurd show of force focused on their campus.

About forty feet from the bonfire, a vacant wooden house stood in a state of neglect. Its falling window shutters, banister railings and rotted loose boards provided the students a rich source of fuel for their bonfire. A joyous Henry Smith, taunting the patrolmen, also ripped down several wooden traffic signposts and tossed them into the fire. A couple of flaming objects were thrown toward the vacant house, though they fizzled out without causing any damage. A flaming signpost ignited a patch of dry grass but did not spread.

Pete Strom, the officer in charge, finally lost patience with Smith and the other students. He summoned a fire truck to douse their bonfire. At 10:30 p.m., the truck, with siren blaring, arrived at the edge of the campus. Highway patrolmen, sixty-six in all, were ordered to protect the firemen as they approached the bonfire. National Guardsmen secured other parts of the area. As the firemen and their patrol guard approached the bonfire, the students moved back toward the dorms, cursing along the way. Several rocks and bottles were thrown toward the firemen from the campus.

While the firemen extinguished the bonfire, two highway patrolmen moved alongside the nearby vacant house that had supplied the firewood. Suddenly, without warning, a heavy white banister came hurtling out of nowhere, hitting one of the patrolmen, David Shealy, in the face. Bleeding profusely from the nose and mouth, Shealy appeared to be seriously wounded. His ghastly appearance spawned confusion and panic among his fellow patrolmen. Rumor quickly spread through the patrol ranks that Shealy had been shot. That's all the tense highway patrolmen needed to hear.

Three patrolmen shouldered their weapons, targeting an embankment near the edge of the campus where most of the students were slowly returning from the site of the bonfire to their dormitories about 400 feet away. Unaware of Shealy's injury and the tension it had caused, some students were embarrassed by their original hasty retreat and began to turn back. "Hey man, they can't do nothing to us on our own campus," one shouted as he reversed direction and moved again toward the armed patrolmen.

Many of the 150 college students on the embankment had never been in a civil rights demonstration before. Realizing they couldn't match the firepower of the police, the students used the best weapon they had— their voices. Ambling back down the hill, some shouted "motherfucker" and "honkies" at the patrolmen below. Others shouted, "Your mama's a whore! Your mama's a whore!"

To the highway patrolmen, the students appeared as ghostly silhouettes set against the darkened campus—the outlines of their bodies dimly illuminated from nearby street lights and the headlamps of police cars. Unbeknownst to the students, their figures were carefully framed through the sights of an arsenal of shotguns, pistols and carbines. When they neared the patrolmen, a shot rang out. Then an intense barrage of gunfire, mostly in the form of deadly buckshot, erupted from the gunmen.

The massacre at Orangeburg lasted about nine seconds. One wounded student described it as like being caught in a wave of falling soldiers, just as in a scene from a war movie. When the shooting ended, three students lay mortally wounded and another twenty-seven had injuries. All but two were shot from the rear or the side as they tried to flee.

Pete Strom, wearing a metal combat helmet, summoned Governor McNair on a direct radio hot line. "Governor," he said, "I'm afraid something terrible has happened."

Chapter 10 — Murder and Denial

"They committed murder. Murder…that's a harsh thing to say, but they did it. The police lost their self control. They just started shooting. It was a slaughter. Double-ought buckshot is what you use for deer. It's meant to kill. One guy emptied his service revolver. That takes a lot of shooting. The [students] are running away. Pow, pow, pow, pow, pow, pow! My God, there's a murderous intent there. We are lucky more weren't killed."

Ramsey Clark, attorney general of the United States in 1968, minced no words when he described what happened in Orangeburg. My journey for answers about the shooting had taken me to his East 12th Street law office in lower Manhattan. I had simply picked up the phone, called, and asked whether he would be willing to answer some questions about the Orangeburg massacre. To my surprise, he consented. Apparently, few others had bothered to ask. I found myself in the presence of one of the few living men in a position to grasp the real story of Orangeburg, and— of equal importance—one who was willing to speak candidly about what he knew.

As the interview began, Clark seemed tentative and somber. He strained to recall the details of the case as he sat at his cluttered wooden desk in a modest office that gave no clue to his earlier years as head of Lyndon Johnson's Justice Department. My initial hopes began to fade. I thought to myself, Orangeburg was one of the hundreds of civil rights cases he had handled in the 1960s. Maybe the details had faded over the decades. But then, as his memory kicked in, Ramsey Clark became increasingly agitated—his outrage gradually returning as he remembered the behavior of South Carolina's officials in the aftermath of the shooting.

The student deaths at Orangeburg were caused by "police criminal acts," he declared, warming quickly to the subject. "The provocation for the incident was an absurd, provocative display of force." He said South Carolina's governor, Robert McNair, responded to Orangeburg with excessive police power because that was the politically expedient thing to do in 1968.

"Fear, anger, a sense of self-righteousness to justify hating began to be seen as successful politics." When the tactic backfired, Clark told me, state officials fabricated stories that many South Carolinians believe to this day. "Part of the reason they put out these stories was shock. We've got these dead bodies on our hands. We can't take this rap."

In the surreal aftermath of the barrage of gunfire, the only certainties were death and injury. Samuel Hammond, age eighteen, a football player, was fatally shot in the back. Delano Middleton, a seventeen-year-old Orangeburg high school student whose mother worked as a maid at the college, died from multiple gunshot wounds. Henry Smith, the exuberant young organizer of the bonfire gathering, was hit from several directions as he was spun around by the intense force of the fusillade. As Smith lay dying on the ground, several patrolmen prodded him with riot sticks, while another struck him with the butt of his gun. Cleveland Sellers, who had joined the rear of the student procession after visiting a nearby dormitory, was shot in the armpit as he tried to help some screaming students escape.

Once again, unhurt students helped the injured get to the campus infirmary. Jordan Simmons, a senior who had been shot in the neck while walking across the campus, hobbled on his own to the infirmary after witnessing the police drag injured students into the darkness. "It was chaos. People were dazed...lying around everywhere in pain. The infirmary had blood all over the floor," Simmons recalled.

Ambulances were prevented from entering the campus. A married and pregnant senior used her car to shuttle the wounded from the infirmary to a nearby Orangeburg hospital. She was stopped by three policemen who beat her and sprayed a chemical in her face. A week later, she suffered a miscarriage. Simmons was lucky to be spotted in the infirmary by his track coach, who drove him to the emergency room.

At the local hospital, a policeman asked, "Who's laughing now?" as he walked smirking past a row of bleeding students in the emergency room. Another officer, when questioned by a hospital employee about what had happened, blurted, "A couple of niggers got stung with birdshot."

As he entered the hospital, the wounded Jordan Simmons remembers hearing a hospital worker use racial epithets as he slowly moved past white men in bibbed overalls wearing badges. "I didn't want to be there," Simmons remembered. "My whole life passed before me. I was alone in that hospital."

His mother, Gladys, didn't want him in that hospital either. Hospital workers, after learning she was the mother of a South Carolina State student, hung up the telephone twice when she called to inquire about her son's condition. She got through only after a helpful telephone company operator intervened.

Told that her son had a fifty-fifty chance of survival, she drove to Orangeburg from her home in Summerville, a town near Charleston. "I was determined if he should die that he have no animosity against his perpetrators," she said. "I didn't want him to die with malice in his heart."

After enduring rude medical personnel and hearing news reports of police beatings upon returning home that night, Mrs. Simmons-Suddeth—whose brother had died in a South Carolina jail years earlier—felt her son was in danger from more than just his gunshot wound. The next day she removed him from the racially hostile environment of the Orangeburg hospital and drove him to Charleston, where he could be under the care of a family physician.

"I was afraid of what they might do. I knew of many cases where they took people out of jail and lynched them. I thought they might do something terrible to Jordan," she said. "It was very barbaric for them to shoot into a bunch of children with buckshot. Then they lied about it. If you are black, whatever *they* say is true. Nobody had any civil rights to fight whatever they said."

After being treated for his wound at the hospital, Cleveland Sellers was arrested. As he was led away by the county sheriff, Sellers—concerned for his own safety—told every student he passed, "Y'all see I'm going with the sheriff. The sheriff's got me." Trained in such survival techniques from his days of civil rights demonstrations in Mississippi, Sellers recalled that his verbal proclamations to witnesses caught the attention of the sheriff and believed they may have kept him alive in the turbulent hours ahead.

The night of February 8 became a "fantasy" born of fear and confusion, Sellers told me in an interview for this book at his childhood home in Demark. Once in custody, he watched a shaken Pete Strom and his colleagues hastily devise a plan to deal with all the chaos swirling around them. "Everyone thought they were in charge, but no one was really in charge. They were real disorganized. It was like watching a slapstick comedy."

Eventually, the white lawmen threw the book at Sellers, charging him with everything they could think of. The final list included arson, inciting a riot, assault and battery with intent to kill, destruction of personal property, damaging real property, housebreaking, and grand larceny. His bond was set at $50,000, a staggering amount for the time. When informed of the charges and the bond amount, Sellers said all he could do was laugh.

As he was paraded in front of television cameras as a police trophy, Sellers smiled. "The smile is the irony of that picture," Sellers recalled. "I could hardly believe what was happening to me. Even though I knew these people were fully capable of all this, it just didn't make any sense."

The night ahead would become even more surreal. The highway patrol closed the entire forty-mile section of Interstate Highway 26 between Orangeburg and Columbia in order to clear the way for the bizarre one-hundred-mile-an-hour midnight ride that would deliver Sellers to the state penitentiary. "They used patrol cars along the way to block access to the Interstate. There was no one on that road but us. That car went so fast it was almost unbelievable. We were flying. To this day, I don't know what they had built up in their minds. These men were nervous and scared. They had completely lost their sense of reality."

Normally, for security reasons, the penitentiary in Columbia is never opened at night. But, as the midnight hour approached on February 8, the state made an exception. When the police car from Orangeburg arrived, the prison warden was waiting. Within minutes, Cleveland Sellers was locked up on death row. "I survived these moments by not trying to make sense of it...by not trying to mentally process it," Sellers said.

It didn't matter that no one had seen any students with guns; no firearms or spent cartridges were found on the campus after the shooting; and a falling wooden banister—not a bullet—had hurt the only injured officer at Orangeburg. It didn't matter that no gunfire had been heard from the South Carolina State campus before the shooting and no warning was given to the students. South Carolina's leaders had their own story—one clearly designed to preserve the state's carefully nurtured image and to protect their own reputations.

In a sweeping misrepresentation of the facts, Governor McNair, Pete Strom and their law enforcement allies led the public to believe a two-way gun battle had taken place in Orangeburg and the loss of life was the fault of the students, not the police. Calling it "one of the saddest days in the history of South Carolina," McNair laid out a remarkable scenario of events at a noon news conference on the day after the shooting.

"The years of work and understanding have been shattered by this unfortunate incident in Orangeburg," McNair told the press. "Our reputation for racial harmony has been blemished by the actions of those who would place selfish motives and interests above the welfare and security of the majority. It has become apparent that the incident last night was sparked by black power advocates who represent only a small minority of the total student bodies at South Carolina State and Claflin. We commend the large portion of the students who remained on the campus and took no part in the violent and provocative demonstrations."

The governor went on. He stated that the confrontation had taken place off campus and that the seriousness of the situation prior to the shooting had been compounded by the theft of firearms from the college's ROTC armory. In fact, every student was shot while on campus and the ROTC break-in occurred more than a half hour *after* the shooting. McNair spoke of a "flammable liquid bomb" used to set fire to a private residence as a provocation. Apparently, he was referring to the vacant house near the bonfire used for firewood. Though flaming objects had been thrown toward the house, the structure did not catch fire. The governor also said the patrolmen fired in response to the wounding of officer Shealy, the man hit by a falling piece of wood near the house. That injury, in fact, occurred a full five minutes before the patrolmen opened fire.

"The actions leading to the three deaths and the numerous injuries came only after an extended period of sniper fire from the campus and not until an officer had been felled during his efforts to protect life and property," McNair told reporters. "Although it was later determined that the patrolman's injury was caused by some type of fallen missile or object, there was reason to believe that at that instant he had been shot. The other patrolmen, with instructions to protect themselves and others, responded with gunfire."

Quietly standing next to the governor as he made these statements was Pete Strom. Many of the factual errors, including the serious contention that a two-way gun battle had taken place in Orangeburg, would never be officially corrected. In fact, both Strom and McNair would repeat the assertions for years to come.

Following the shooting, the governor appointed Henry Lake, his former legal aide and a onetime highway patrolman, as the official spokesman for matters involving Orangeburg. Lake, who carried a snub-nosed .38 pistol in his belt, had no criticism of his former patrol colleagues but plenty for the "outside agitator" he blamed for the deaths. Accusing Cleveland Sellers of throwing the banister that hit Patrolman Shealy, Lake said, "He's the main man. He's the biggest nigger in the crowd."

Nathaniel Abraham, a black journalist who wandered among the highway patrolmen in the minutes preceding the shooting, is one of the few eyewitnesses who was in a position to dispute the official story. His account, however, is highly controversial and disbelieved by some journalists, including Jack Bass, co-author of *The Orangeburg Massacre*.

Abraham, in an interview for this book, told me that Pete Strom lied about the series of events that led up to the shooting. Sensing that an attack on the campus was inevitable, Abraham said he warned some of the students on the embankment that the patrolmen were almost surely going to strike. Just before the gunfire erupted, Abraham said, he approached Strom, grabbed his arm and pleaded with him that shooting the students was unnecessary.

"You're too late, nigger, get up there where you belong," Abraham quoted Strom, who was "suggesting" that the journalist go up on the embankment to join the students. At that moment, Abraham said, Strom raised a carbine. "He aimed it point-blank at me. It was so close it touched my chest. I slapped it out of his hand and ran."

After the carbine hit the ground, Abraham said Strom picked up the weapon and fired it in his direction. "He tried to kill me," Abraham claimed. Almost simultaneously the attack on the students began. "I ran through the dark on my hands and knees with bullets flying over my head," Abraham recalled.

Investigations into the shooting followed, the most prominent launched immediately by the FBI on the order of Attorney General Clark. South Carolina officials publicly pledged cooperation. Governor McNair urged quick public disclosure of the FBI findings. In a statement, the governor said "a full disclosure of the facts is essential because of the concern and confusion over the tragedy and because of the pressing urgency that the facts in this matter be made public."

The governor promised that a full report of the activities of Pete Strom's police agency, the State Law Enforcement Division (SLED), and the South Carolina Highway Patrol "will be submitted and a subsequent full factual disclosure of these reports will also be made public as soon thereafter as possible."

It was all a charade.

Chapter 11 — The Cover-Up

After nearly thirty-five years, Robert McNair has yet to reveal to the public the results of any investigation of the Orangeburg massacre. He refused to allow journalists Bass and Nelson to examine the report of Strom's SLED, if there ever was one. The head of the highway patrol said his agency made no investigation or report because it didn't want to interfere with the FBI investigation.

The governor also refused to name a special blue ribbon committee to investigate Orangeburg because he said Negroes would be suspicious of anyone he appointed. Yet, soon after, he refused to cooperate with an attempt by the University of South Carolina to study what happened at Orangeburg.

The governor's lack of cooperation with any serious investigation was made possible by his widespread public support among the white voters of South Carolina. These constituents, the ones that really mattered to the governor, bought his story. The state's conservative news media, a timid group that generally accepted McNair's public statements at face value, did no independent investigation. Within McNair's political base, there was simply no demand for accountability. Bass and Nelson quoted an unidentified college friend of McNair who watched the governor's explanation of the Orangeburg shooting on television. Turning to his wife, the man said, "I don't know who put that (story) together, but they did a damn good job. Nobody'll ever know exactly what happened, but Bobby'll come out smelling like a rose."

One who didn't buy Robert McNair's story was Ramsey Clark. With Orangeburg, the attorney general found that investigating the crimes of law enforcement officers can be a Byzantine task. Over time, Clark learned that FBI agents purposely misled the Justice Department about important details in the Orangeburg case; that key evidence was severely compromised by FBI agents friendly with Pete Strom and his men; and that his own U.S. attorney, based in Columbia, would not cooperate with the investigation. The extent of the law enforcement corruption reached new heights one day when Robert Owen, the second-highest-ranking official in the Justice Department's civil rights division, sought out Charles DeFord, the agent-in-charge of the FBI office in Columbia. DeFord, to Owen's astonishment, was at the Holiday Inn in Orangeburg sharing a room with none other than Pete Strom, the key subject of the investigation.

McNair's promise of cooperation to Clark also proved hollow. The governor's pledge that he would instruct the patrolmen who were on the scene to give statements to the federal government extended only to the compromised FBI agents the patrolmen already knew as law enforcement cronies. Strom's state police officers, the highway patrol and Orangeburg police all refused to give interviews to anyone except their friends at the FBI.

Ultimately, with little evidence and the lack of support of his local U.S. attorney, a federal grand jury in South Carolina refused to indict the highway patrolmen who shot the students. McNair was quick to portray the grand jury's failure to bring charges as an exoneration of the patrol's actions. He expressed hope this would "put an end to the speculation and uncertainty surrounding the incident."

Acknowledging it would be an uphill battle to convict the highway patrolmen in South Carolina, the Justice Department immediately filed its own criminal charges against the gunmen. The government alleged that nine patrolmen fired their weapons at the students "with the intent of imposing summary punishment," thus depriving them of "life or liberty without due process of law."

At the time, the charge was a misdemeanor and carried a maximum penalty of a year in prison and a $1,000 fine. (Later, the penalty for the same crime was raised to life imprisonment if the victim died.) The Justice Department felt it had a good case and an obligation to present the evidence against the patrolmen in open court. "It was our duty to enforce the law," said Clark. "If it seemed to us to be an important violation, we had an obligation to proceed even if we thought we might not win the case. If the juries won't convict, it's their responsibility. But I'm not doing my duty if I don't prosecute where I have a case."

The trial, held in the town of Florence, brought a rehash of the state's now familiar refrain. The patrolmen fired, their attorney argued, in their own self-defense preceding "a highly dangerous, explosive, riotous situation" caused by an outside agitator. At the time the patrolmen fired, said defense attorney J. C. Coleman, several hundred persons were "thundering at them, coming at them, charging, hurling brickbats, hurling pieces of concrete. Our evidence will show there was shooting at that time from that group." Some thirty-six witnesses testified for the prosecution, including students, newsmen, a fireman, three highway patrolmen, two National Guardsmen and three FBI agents.

In his instructions to the jury, the judge said that the prosecution must prove beyond a reasonable doubt that the patrolmen fired in anger and not in fear. Thus, the jury was asked to decide whether or not they believed the patrolmen acted in self-defense and believed they were in imminent danger when they opened fire.

In the jury room, the ten white members were ready to render an immediate verdict, having no doubt that the patrolmen had acted in self-defense. The two black jurors raised questions. It didn't take long, however, for the black members of the panel to be drawn to the prevailing view, noted one of the white jurors after the proceeding. "They seemed to understand when we explained," juror James T. Hollar of Columbia, told Bass and Nelson. The jury reached its decision in less than half an hour, but Hollar said the court "asked us to stay in longer, rather than walk out so quickly."

State officials claimed the jury verdict exonerated their actions in Orangeburg. The head of the state highway patrol said there would be no changes in the patrol's riot control tactics. In fact, five of the defendant patrolmen had received promotions in rank before the trial. One of the patrolmen who fired on the students was promoted in 1987 to the top job of commander of the highway patrol.

All that remained was the prosecution of Cleveland Sellers. Finally free from South Carolina jails on reduced bail, the activist was ordered not to come within five miles of Orangeburg. This meant he could not even retrieve his personal effects from the small frame house he had used as a residence during the demonstrations. During the two-year period before the trial, Sellers's possessions disappeared, including photographs and personal memorabilia from his civil rights days in Mississippi.

Though Attorney General Clark said he saw no evidence that Cleveland Sellers had anything to do with the Orangeburg demonstrations other than getting shot, South Carolina's officials were not about to let him go. Most of the original charges concocted by the lawmen on the night of the shooting were dropped. An Orangeburg grand jury, however, ultimately indicted Sellers for participating in a riot, incitement to riot, and conspiracy to incite others to riot.

A little over a year after the highway patrolmen were acquitted, the Sellers trial began in Orangeburg with the same overblown display of police power exhibited in the demonstrations that started it all. The streets outside the courthouse were barricaded. Nearly forty highway patrol cars were prominently parked in a nearby motel parking lot. At least one hundred National Guardsmen were placed on standby alert.

In a not-so-subtle attempt at law enforcement intimidation, twenty armed highway patrolmen sat shoulder-to-shoulder across the front row of the two-hundred-seat spectator's gallery in the Orangeburg courtroom. Yet, after hearing ten prosecution witnesses unable to connect Sellers to the events of the night of February 8, the judge dismissed the two remaining charges involving the campus massacre. A single riot charge, relating to the bowling alley protest, was left to stand.

When testimony began, Orangeburg police chief Poston and Pete Strom painted Sellers as a troublemaker. For over four hours, Poston described the demonstration, testifying that he saw Sellers "move from group to group" in front of Harry Floyd's bowling alley. When Sellers finished talking, each group became more agitated, he said. However, on cross-examination, Poston said Sellers had appeared peaceful and orderly and had committed no illegal acts on the night of the protest. As to what Sellers had said to the groups of students, Poston admitted he had heard not a single word.

Strom testified that he witnessed Sellers "violating many laws." When Seller's attorney, Howard Moore, asked Strom to cite some specific legal violations, the crusty old lawman hesitated and then said, "He refused to disperse immediately when ordered by Chief Poston. That's a violation."

The defense presented no witnesses, convinced that the state had failed to make its case against Cleveland Sellers. The mostly white Orangeburg jury—bombarded with frightening rumors from law enforcement officials about Sellers for two years—felt otherwise. After just over two hours of deliberations, they found him guilty. The judge imposed the maximum sentence of one year's imprisonment and a $250 fine.

South Carolina had nailed its scapegoat.

Chapter 12 — The Fallout

As a young reporter for United Press International based in Mississippi during the waning days of the civil rights era, I witnessed first-hand how the movement of the 1960s caused significant changes in racial attitudes throughout much of the South. The turmoil over civil rights forced white citizens in countless communities to face segregation head-on and begin to deal with the vast problems of racial inequality. The struggle spawned a more honest, racially sensitive political climate in many places. South Carolina, unfortunately, was not one of them.

The state's self-image as a haven of racial tranquility has always been a façade. Rather than genuinely face its long-festering racial problems, South Carolina's avoidance of high-profile civil rights conflicts allowed it to elude the introspection needed to wrestle with the serious issues that have long divided the races. Its "New South" mask concealed the state's special brand of aristocratic, paternal racism that has long thrived in a culture where blacks are widely regarded as uneducated, second-class citizens who depend on white benevolence to survive. Since such a paternalistic society places a high value on stability and maintaining class distinctions, it's easy to understand the need to blame an "outside agitator" when the illusion of normalcy is suddenly pierced.

Scapegoating, in fact, has been integral to white Southern culture since the slave insurrection scares of the pre-Civil War era. In his book, *Honor and Violence in the Old South*, Bertram Wyatt-Brown described a process of ferreting out rebel slaves that bears an uncanny resemblance to official South Carolina's handling of the Orangeburg shootings. "The process took the form of mass ritual: the initial discovery of the plot, the arousal of public opinion to the danger, the naming of conspirators through informers and trials, the setting of penalties, sometimes reviews by state authorities, the final disposition of the prisoners and the relaxation of agitation," wrote Wyatt-Brown.

In the antebellum years—just as in 1968—perceptions of social imbalance led to frantic demands for group conformity to the traditional moral values. During the time of slavery, wrote Wyatt-Brown, the obvious purpose was "the allegiance demanded of all to white-race superiority and the obligation of all to ferret out those who threatened the social structure through secret malevolence. Whether there by self-selection, as rebel leaders, or by white scapegoating of innocents, blacks in the dock for conspiracy and treason were despised as symbols of all that was evil."

For such occasions, Southern society had to have its ready supply of victims—individuals who Wyatt-Brown said were deviants by choice or by public decree. "They provided the standard of unacceptable conduct, making clear what rules could not be broken without reprisal. As the insurrectionary ceremonies attested, the powerless and guiltless were most often the subjects of popular sacrifice."

When one carefully reviews the words and actions of Governor McNair and his law enforcement representatives in 1968, it's hard to miss the similarity of the Orangeburg massacre to the handling of plantation uprisings a century and a half earlier. McNair's emphasis on maintaining order by building up massive displays of armed force; the repeated use of the word "control" when referring to the conduct of the black students; the call for public and media unanimity against a common enemy; and, of course, the scapegoating of an innocent (Cleveland Sellers), who becomes a symbol of evil.

When the plan goes wrong, those responsible shift blame to others, decry the damage to the community and their own image and reputations, create an elaborate cover-up of the truth to distort history, and then enter a lifelong period of denial. Southern values are at stake, and honor must be maintained.

In the months following the Orangeburg shooting, officials in South Carolina attempted to make amends to the black community. A court ordered Harry Floyd to open his All Star Bowling Lanes to black customers. Floyd did as ordered, and John Stroman, the young bowler who led the first demonstration, eventually became one of his best customers. "Ol' Harry Floyd is all right," Stroman told a *Washington Post* reporter in 1978. "He's changed his views, you know."

The South Carolina legislature opened the public coffers to South Carolina State, helping it finance a new round of campus construction. One of those new buildings, a facility for athletic and other college events, was named Smith-Hammond-Middleton Memorial Center to honor the slain students. Another, the Martin Luther King Jr. Auditorium, is the site of an annual memorial service in remembrance of the tragedy.

Though the state responded to the crisis with increased funding for what is now South Carolina State University, it never officially admitted culpability in the campus shooting. The many investigations and reports promised by the governor never materialized. Governor McNair, after dismissing the Bass-Nelson book as "more fiction than fact," began a long public silence on the subject of Orangeburg.

In the summer of 1992, McNair—then head of one of the state's largest and most politically connected law firms—agreed to meet with me in his office on an "off the record" basis. There would be no formal interview, just a brief meeting to say hello. The meeting was arranged by a former colleague who knew McNair well and had stayed in touch with him over the years. It had been about twenty-five years since I'd been in McNair's presence and I suspected that outside of my work on the Orangeburg story the former governor didn't remember me at all.

A few years earlier I had written and directed a public radio drama based on the Bass-Nelson book and the role of Governor McNair was played by James Whitmore, the distinguished actor nominated for an Academy Award for his performance as Harry S. Truman in *Give 'Em Hell, Harry!* It was well known that McNair had not been pleased about the publicity surrounding this nationally-broadcast dramatization of the Orangeburg shooting. It had fueled new public discussion about a story that he wished would fade away. This time I was in the early stages of research for this book and I suspect McNair had agreed to our meeting simply because he wanted to size up someone he considered to be a continuing source of irritation.

In my presence McNair never let on that Orangeburg mattered much to him at all. He greeted me warmly in his elegant private office just across the street from South Carolina's state capitol. He is known personally to be a gracious, cordial, hospitable man—one capable of making anyone, even an adversary, feel comfortable. That old saying—he could charm a cat off of a shrimp boat—applies perfectly to this easygoing politician.

But underneath this amiable veneer, McNair remained unresponsive on Orangeburg. After the small talk turned to the shooting, he reminded me that he was sticking to his "no interview" position. He did, however, maintain that he'd done the right things in Orangeburg.

Offering no explanation of the many glaring discrepancies in his public statements following the shooting, McNair suggested that I read an oral history covering his tenure in office recorded in 1979 by the University of South Carolina for the state archives. That's all he had to offer on the subject. Our meeting ended as it began—polite banter without substance.

I took the governor's advice and visited the reading room at the South Carolina archives. What I found was irritating, though it shouldn't have surprised me. After spending a full day reviewing transcripts of various interviews on the McNair years, it became obvious that a key goal of this oral history was to sanitize McNair's involvement in the events leading up to the Orangeburg violence. The university's interviewers played softball with their subjects, not challenging statements that conflicted with well-known evidence. It was another whitewash.

For example, an interview on March 24, 1979 with Pete Strom was rife with misstated information and errors in facts. Strom confused the student-built bonfire—a threat to no one—with the nearby vacant house, which he claimed was "set on fire." The house never burned. "We decided, as a matter of public policy, we couldn't let anyone burn...a private dwelling," Strom stated. Going further, he said: "As the fire truck started pouring water on the fire, someone threw a banister and hit one of the patrolmen right in the face and that set it off...because they was already shooting." In fact, there was no shooting on the campus until the patrolmen opened fire on the students a full five minutes later.

Unfortunately, the years would not give Strom a chance to have a change of heart about his story. He died in 1989, still head of the state police, his reputation as "Mr. Law Enforcement" having reached legendary status in South Carolina.

For whatever reason, McNair's own recorded story in the oral history is sealed and unavailable to the public. Whether he shed new light on the shooting in his recorded memoir is not known. However, the kid glove treatment given McNair's associates by the university interviewers does not suggest the governor was challenged for serious answers. The entire McNair oral history project was not only a sad example of shoddy scholarship under the sponsorship of the University of South Carolina, but its misrepresentations served to distort history and make it more difficult for future researchers to get at the truth.

The former governor did, however, revisit the subject of Orangeburg in an interview with Harriet Keyserling, a former member of the South Carolina House of Representatives, for her 1998 memoir, *Against the Tide*. Again, McNair repeated much of his original story—even parts long ago discredited.

In the interview conducted in early 1998, McNair told Keyserling he did not go to Orangeburg on the advice of Pete Strom. During the crisis, however, he said he met often in Columbia with black and white leaders in an attempt to resolve the issues. McNair said they were on the verge of an agreement "when the last riot erupted." The former governor then repeated, according to sections paraphrased in the book, two erroneous elements of the state's earlier story: First, "The troops had been withdrawn from the scene, but when the fire department, called to come back a third time to put out new fires in the burning house, refused to come without police protection, the troops rushed back." (Again, the house was not on fire; the troops were not withdrawn.) Second, McNair described the students' actions as a riot led by outside agitators that had to be quelled. (There was no student riot and there were no outside agitators.)

Chad Quaintance, lead prosecutor for the Justice Department in the trial against the highway patrolmen, was especially surprised to hear that Strom and McNair had cited a burning house as a provocation for the shooting. "Memory can do funny things to people," Quaintance said in an interview. "The house was not on fire. I saw the house (after the shooting). There was no evidence to suggest that and it was never an issue. No one contended at the trial that the house was on fire."

Besides the slain students and their families, no one suffered more from the events at Orangeburg than South Carolina's scapegoat, Cleveland Sellers. After exhausting his appeals, Sellers served seven months of his one-year sentence on the charge of participating in the bowling alley riot. Upon his release, the director of South Carolina's Department of Corrections, William Leake, referred to Sellers as "a political prisoner." Soft-spoken and thoughtful about his Orangeburg experience, Sellers told the *Charlotte Observer* he was feared in 1968 because "I posed a threat to the civility that the state wanted to hide behind—[the idea] that everything was fine."

During the period between his conviction and final appeal, Sellers earned a master's degree in education at Harvard University. Later, he earned a doctorate in education administration from the University of North Carolina in Greensboro. He wanted to be a college teacher, but the ghosts of Orangeburg haunted him for the next quarter century. "I filed [teaching] applications all over the place, but Orangeburg just killed that," Sellers said in a newspaper interview. "Administrators felt I represented some kind of threat to the stability of their institutions."

Unable to secure a teaching position, Sellers worked for the City of Greensboro for seventeen years, holding jobs with youth employment services, city planning, and public housing. Upon the death of both his parents in 1990, he returned to his childhood home in Denmark to manage his family's rental properties and teach a few classes at Denmark Technical College. Back in his home town, he became active with community groups, worked with children, and served for several years on the state board of education.

In late 1992, as the twenty-fifth anniversary of the massacre approached, a series of events began that would eventually free Cleveland Sellers from the legal stigma of Orangeburg. Jack Bass, *The Orangeburg Massacre* co-author and then professor of journalism at the University of Mississippi, approached his old friend, Rhett Jackson, owner of South Carolina's largest independent bookstore and a former president of the American Booksellers Association. Jackson was a member and past chairman of the South Carolina Probation, Pardon and Parole Board.

In most states, the governor holds the authority to pardon. In South Carolina, that power rests with the seven-member board on which Jackson served. Bass asked Jackson whether he thought it was possible that the board might pardon Sellers. "I thought they probably would," Jackson recalled, that is, if Sellers submitted a formal application requesting the pardon.

"I agreed with Jack Bass that Cleveland Sellers wasn't guilty of anything other than being set-up with the Jim Crow laws and being fed up with the injustice of watching his mother and father not have equal treatment and facilities in the world," Jackson said. "If I'd been a young man and black at that time, I'd have been there with him."

After submission of all the paperwork and a positive field investigation by the board's staff, Jackson quietly lobbied the board's six other members for support of the Sellers application. "I found mostly a good attitude. Two or three members didn't know much about it. It had been twenty-five years. I wanted the state to say 'We're sorry. Here's a pardon, let's erase [the conviction].' It was time to tell this man to live his life. I told the other members the state could have charged another hundred students with the same offense, but they had to have some scapegoat. Cleveland just happened to be the one because he was visible."

Luckily, South Carolina's news media failed to learn of the efforts to pardon Sellers until just before the scheduled vote. With no adverse publicity and little time for controversy to build against the proposed pardon, the board voted its unanimous approval on July 20, 1993.

After the pardon was granted, Jackson received only one negative phone call. It was from a man who said he was in law enforcement during the time of the shooting. The board, he insisted, didn't know the whole story of what had happened in Orangeburg. When Jackson asked for his name, the man refused to identify himself. The caller did, however, have a question about Sellers. "What's that 'boy' doing now?" he asked. "Boy!" Jackson barked into the phone. "Are you speaking of Doctor Cleveland Sellers?" The man hung up.

As legal forgiveness from the state, the pardon given Cleveland Sellers was the first and only formal acknowledgement by a governmental body in South Carolina that all was not right with the official version of the events in Orangeburg. One of the key reasons the state has failed to come to grips with Orangeburg, Jackson surmised, is that former Governor McNair and the law enforcement community still feel a deep guilt over the deaths of the students.

"To say 'I was wrong' are three very difficult words," said Jackson. "I think the law enforcement people must have some guilt about the shotguns they had loaded with buckshot. Or the story that they were fired on first, which was absolutely proven not to be so. They are just trying to protect themselves. It's an old story and they want their version to stand [as history]. But it's not the true version."

Though Jackson said that he's known Robert McNair most of his life, he has never spoken with the former governor about the shooting. "He's a decent man, he's got a good heart, and he was moving to be a real moderate in race relations," said Jackson. "I think this thing just happened, and he didn't think it through clearly. He believed what Strom and the others were telling him. If in the end, he'd just said publicly that he didn't handle it right he might have gained a lot of respect from the black community.

"But he was close to Pete Strom and it was just easier later on not to deal with it and to try to shift the blame," Jackson continued. "All human beings get in that situation sometimes. They regret how they handled something, but they just can't correct it. They can't say 'I was wrong.'"

John West, McNair's lieutenant governor and successor as governor, said his former colleague has "agonized" for years over the Orangeburg killings. "Orangeburg has been a very, very sensitive part of his life," West said of McNair. "I know it has caused him a great deal of grief and concern. I'm very sympathetic with Bob McNair about the Orangeburg situation."

As to the continuing holes in official accounts of Orangeburg, West said, "Given the circumstances of the times, the inconsistencies are perhaps more understandable. There was a feeling among most law enforcement officers that segregation should be maintained."

Jordan Simmons, a corporate computer executive after a long career in the military, saw the continuing denial over the facts of Orangeburg as similar to the repeated claims that the Holocaust never occurred during World War II. "Regardless of the proof and all the evidence, there are still those who claim the Holocaust didn't happen," said Simmons, who, in his mid-fifties, still has fragments of highway patrol buckshot in his neck. "It makes them feel comfortable; it makes them feel secure. It removes a sense of guilt. It's a natural tendency for people who experience something hurtful to try to deny it. But eventually they have to face up to it to get well."

Former attorney general Ramsey Clark agreed that on a personal level
McNair probably has never put the tragedy of Orangeburg behind him.
"Governor McNair had political ambitions that made him want to be
seen as a very strong governor," Clark said. "Therefore he had to show
these [demonstrators] that they had to behave themselves in his state. He,
like some other governors at the time, wanted the feds to solve their
racial problems. They didn't want to take the heat. Orangeburg changed
McNair. He was badly hurt by it, just as [former Michigan governor]
George Romney was hurt by the Detroit riots. I don't think they ever get
over it."

Chapter 13 — The Struggle to Shape History

Eight years after his pardon and more than three decades after being shot, on a day that Cleveland Sellers could only describe as "mind boggling," came proof that miracles do happen. It was about noon, April 6, 2000. Over 2,000 people—white, black, rich and poor—gathered at the end of a five-day march from Charleston to Columbia to force the removal of the Confederate flag from the dome of the South Carolina capitol.

The protest march ended with the remarkable image of Cleveland Sellers standing outside in the crowded statehouse plaza alongside the current Democratic governor of South Carolina, Jim Hodges, and his Republican predecessor, David Beasley. Charleston Mayor Joseph Riley, speaking to the cheering crowd, hailed fellow marcher Sellers—now on the faculty at the University of South Carolina—as a "wonderful civil rights leader." Then the mayor noted that his own son viewed Sellers as a hero.

"I had to pinch myself," a giddy Sellers said after the ceremony in which he was finally recognized and embraced publicly by the state's political leaders. "We are witnessing South Carolina's coming into the civil rights era. Unfortunately, we've come in at the beginning of the twenty-first century. But it's important that we've started to come."

The irony of watching a broad cross section of South Carolinians use the protest march—a core tactic of the civil rights movement—was impossible to miss, especially to a seasoned organizer like Sellers. "It just says the tactics that were employed in the civil rights movement were tactics that are generic—anybody can use them in order to register their complaint. It's interesting that we're in the year 2000 and we have to use our feet again."

Absent from the march and rally protesting the Confederate flag was former governor McNair, a man with whom Sellers had by now spoken with on several occasions about the events at Orangeburg. "I've addressed my differences with him," said Sellers. "I've raised the issues and I've tried to make clear what happened. Now, it's up to him and others to decide."

It appears that McNair decided, at least privately, that Sellers was not the dangerous "outside agitator" that he publicly blamed for causing the violence in Orangeburg. In January, 2001—during an outdoor campus luncheon following a celebration of the two hundredth anniversary of the University of South Carolina—Sellers dined with McNair and his wife at the former governor's table.

As John West, McNair's successor, approached, the former governor rose to introduce Sellers to West. "Do you know my friend Cleveland Sellers?" McNair asked West. "Delighted to see you," a surprised West responded.

"I didn't know [Sellers] previously," recalled West. "But I recognized the name very well. I thought it was a rather neat sort of situation."

A month later, however, at the thirty-third anniversary of the shooting, Sellers made it clear that old wounds remain open. As he spoke to a memorial assembly on the Orangeburg campus—one that included Gov. Hodges—the activist broke down and turned away from the audience. Embraced and comforted by his fellow shooting victim, Jordan Simmons, a shaken Sellers returned to the lectern, speaking again after the crowd rose to cheer for him to continue.

"For years the state and the nation have been silent about the Orangeburg tragedy," Sellers said haltingly. "Some of us remain in a state of denial concerning the truth. We must tell the truth of this tragedy. We should no longer blame the victims."

Fighting back tears, Sellers proceeded slowly.

"Truth comes to us from the past—like gold washed down from the mountains. The only way we find the truth is to examine the past honestly. [The year 1968] for me was massive distortion, criminal injustice, and persecution. I was vilified and made to feel like a predator."

"For the past thirty-three years, the struggle for justice and equality has continued to rage inside of me. I don't look back with pity. I know that we were right. I'm not angry because I know justice will prevail. Today we come to ease our hearts and souls...by showing our humanity. We have also come to tell our stories."

And tell their stories, they did. During a day of remembrances, many of the victims of the Orangeburg shooting—men now in their 50s—sat in front of video cameras to bare their souls for a new oral history project on the massacre. Finally, after three decades, the victims of Orangeburg recorded their personal stories for the ages.

Charles Hildebrand, age fifty-two, shot four times on the night of February 8, said that the oral history will help counter the state's "official" version of events for historians in the future. "From the standpoint of history and being able to tell your own story, this oral history is very important," Hildebrand said. "If you look at the some of the newspaper accounts during that time, the story of Orangeburg has been misrepresented."

In an effort to balance the many one-sided accounts of the shooting by supporters of Robert McNair, transcripts of the students' oral history interviews will be deposited in several libraries and archives throughout the state. South Carolina State University and the Avery Research Center at College of Charleston will maintain the original tape recordings.

"We wanted to bring some perspective to what happened on the campus that night, and the days before and after," said Bill Hine, a history professor at South Carolina State and director of the oral history project. "Even though thirty years have passed, we felt there was still much information that could be gleaned from people who had not previously been interviewed or made any public statement about the events in 1968."

Hine expressed optimism that the oral history would provide an accurate accounting of what happened on the night of February 8. "Though there has never been any evidence to support it, there are still people who believe the students were armed, raging militants about to burn down the town," said Hine. "I think this oral history shows this was not the case."

Coincidentally, the day the former students recorded their history was also a day that provided a rare glimpse at the way South Carolina's mainstream media establishment has tried to shape the Orangeburg story over the years. The incident occurred at *The State*, a newspaper established in 1891 as—according to its own corporate history—"a voice in opposition" to "dishonest and incompetent" political bosses. In 1986, *The State*, now South Carolina's largest newspaper, was purchased by Knight-Ridder Corporation.

News columnist John Monk, a leading journalist at the venerable daily, used the thirty-third anniversary of the Orangeburg shooting to write that former governor McNair had "presided over a whitewash" of the facts surrounding the tragedy.

In a prominent front-page article, Monk noted that Gov. Hodges, the first chief executive to attend the annual Orangeburg memorial event, had broken new ground by uttering the word *massacre* when he referred to the shooting. By using the word in his speech, Monk wrote, Hodges "acknowledged state law officers were wrong to gun down defenseless black students."

Monk also highlighted the difference in language used by McNair and the incumbent governor in describing the events at Orangeburg. "Instead of calling the slain students 'agitators' (as McNair had), Hodges referred to them as 'brave young men' seeking to exercise basic rights," Monk wrote.

The respected journalist acknowledged for the first time on the pages of the *The State* that the young activist Cleveland Sellers had been made the "scapegoat" for Orangeburg. He also noted McNair's absence at the Orangeburg ceremony, and quoted Charita Drummond, age nineteen, who said, "The old governor, I guess what happened really didn't mean much to him. He never came to pay his respects."

John Monk's article, published on February 9, 2001, the day after the ceremony, hit the newspaper's conservative readers like a bomb. For the first time in more than three decades, the newspaper had challenged the official version of the white establishment's role in the police violence. Irate calls and letters shook the newsroom in Columbia.

The first indication that an editorial meltdown was occurring within the newspaper came when Monk's story was not posted on *The State's* Web site. Then, without even speaking with John Monk directly about his article, *The State's* publisher, Fred Mott, began his own damage control. He picked up the phone and called Robert McNair to apologize.

"I think [Monk's article] was flat one-sided and, quite frankly, an embarrassment to this newspaper," Mott said in an interview for this book. "I thought the way he went about it was unprofessional. He used some loaded words. So I called Governor McNair and said 'I'm sorry.'"

As Mott discussed the story, he became increasingly agitated. "What Monk did in his article was to take specific pieces that fit how he wanted to view [the events at Orangeburg] and use it to pat our current governor on the back and carry out a whitewash [of his own] of what all the facts were," Mott said.

The State's publisher strongly challenged the use of the word *massacre* in describing the Orangeburg shooting. "That word is inflammatory," he said. "Anytime you use loaded words [in describing] a high-ranking former official, it's something that needs to be looked at and edited carefully." He added that the newspaper's editors had let the article slip by without proper scrutiny because "it's politically correct to take the view that John Monk did."

When asked if he'd personally studied the facts surrounding the Orangeburg shooting, Mott began a clumsy account of events in 1968 that appeared to mix up the activities of John Stroman, the man who organized the original bowling alley protest, and Cleveland Sellers, the activist who was shot by highway patrolmen.

Much of his personal information on the shooting, Mott said, was acquired from the writings of South Carolina historian Walter Edgar, who heads the Institute for Southern Studies at the University of South Carolina. Edgar's 716-page *South Carolina: A History*, published in 1998, devotes a mere two paragraphs—less than half a page—to the Orangeburg shooting. That book, Edgar's office confirmed, is the only work in which the historian has written about the violence at Orangeburg.

Edgar, who avoided the use of the word *massacre* in his book, reports that "three young men fell, mortally wounded" on the night of February 8, but makes no mention that twenty-seven others were shot by white highway patrolmen. After the shooting, McNair and other state leaders "worked diligently to restore trust and good will," Edgar wrote.

In a written response for this book, John Monk addressed his publisher's criticism of the Orangeburg column: "Clearly, Mr. Mott and I differ on this one. It's only fair to point out, however, that under Mr. Mott, I and other writers at *The State* have freedom to write on a wide variety of controversial topics. Under Mr. Mott, *The State*—though not perfect—is by far the most progressive, thorough and aggressive newspaper in South Carolina."

As the Orangeburg story evolved through its fourth decade, efforts intensified to influence the public record for future historians. At the same time former students recorded their accounts for history, former governor McNair was hard at work with a writer on a planned book that would focus on his years in public office. The Modern Political Collection at the University of South Carolina announced plans to create an Internet-based interactive retrospective of McNair's years in office.

In the meantime, a vigorous examination of racial issues continued on the campus of the University of South Carolina. As undergraduate director of USC's African-American Studies Program, Cleveland Sellers taught classes on the history of black Americans and the civil rights movement. Here, nobody tried to whitewash the story of Orangeburg. The classes of Professor Sellers proved so popular that a waiting list formed for admission.

Highway patrolmen seconds before opening
fire on students in Orangeburg on Feb. 8, 1968.

(Photo by Dean Livingston)

Mortally wounded students after the shooting
by highway patrolmen on Feb. 8, 1968.

(Photo by Bill Barley ©1968)

Firemen douse student bonfire just before highway
patrolmen open fire in Orangeburg.

(Photos by Bill Barley ©1968)

Cleveland Sellers (center) after his arrest on the night
of Feb. 8, 1968. Pete Strom (left), in combat helmet, after
charging Sellers with a litany of crimes.

Gov. Robert McNair meets students to discuss Orangeburg
in his office on March 13, 1968. Armed gunman were hidden from
view in the next room to protect the governor in case of violence.

(Photo by Bill Barley ©1968)

Gov. Robert McNair   Attorney General
1968   Ramsey Clark, 1968

Pete Strom   Cleveland Sellers
Portrait from the 1960s   April 6, 2000

(Photo by Jim Covington)

Rhett Jackson (left), John Monk (center) and Jack Bass
in Orangeburg on Feb. 8, 2001. The next day
Monk's controversial article would appear in
The State Newspaper.

(Photo by Jim Covington)

Part Three

No Direction Home

Chapter 14 — Honea Path: An Old Secret Revealed

In a midnight phone call in November, 1994, I got the history lesson of a lifetime.

The caller was Jack Bass, co-author of *The Orangeburg Massacre*. He was in Atlanta, and had just returned from a preview screening of a new documentary film, *The Uprising of '34*.

"Are you related to Dan Beacham, the man who ran the Chiquola Mill in Honea Path in the 1930s?" he asked with a tinge of alarm in his voice.

"Yes, he was my grandfather," I mumbled, trying wake up and shake off the sleep I'd just begun.

"Do you know what happened there?" he prodded gently.

"Not really. Only that there was some kind of violent labor dispute. I could never get anybody to tell me the whole story."

"Well, you've got to see this movie as soon as you can," Bass insisted.

The next morning I called the production office of *The Uprising of '34*, which happened to be a few blocks away from my home in New York City. I told them my story and quickly received a video cassette of the documentary. After watching the tape, I sat frozen. I was stunned by what I had learned, yet angry at how it had been revealed to me. A new window to my childhood years in the South had sprung open and I was appreciative for that. *Uprising* brought clarity to a taboo subject on which I had only vague previous knowledge. Once again the South had spilled her secrets to me in a strange way.

That forbidden subject was a riot that erupted at the local textile mill in my hometown of Honea Path, South Carolina, on the morning of September 6, 1934. Friends and neighbors came to blows in a labor dispute. When it was over, seven people were dead and thirty others wounded.

My grandfather, Dan Beacham, was the mayor of the town and the superintendent of Chiquola Manufacturing Company, operator of the cotton mill where the violence occurred. Since he died in 1936 and my birth came in 1948, I never knew him. My limited knowledge of his life came only through family stories about him, which, at best, were superficial. It would not be until 1994, long after the death of nearly all of the family members who knew him, that I would finally be exposed to an important fact: my grandfather organized the posse of gunmen who opened fire on their fellow workers at Chiquola, and played a major role in engineering a cover-up of the event that lasted nearly six decades.

The bloody riot at the town's cotton mill on that Thursday morning in 1934 shaped the lives of two generations to follow—not because of the shock of what was known—but by what was unknown. Threats and intimidation were used to silence the greatest tragedy in the town's history. A cruel camouflage of fear suffocated the community for almost sixty years.

The killings in Honea Path were the direct result of intense passions that arose during the General Textile Strike that swept the South in 1934. Although the historical facts seem clear, it was difficult for me—having been raised in this tiny community of little more than two thousand people—to understand how a disagreement over labor practices, no matter how intense, could drive neighbors to turn on one another with deadly force. Even more difficult to comprehend was how an event of such magnitude could have been hidden for over half a century.

I also could not escape the irony that I first learned of my grandfather's role from Jack Bass. Of all people, Bass—a reporter who had unearthed the dark secrets of the Orangeburg massacre—was telling me of another Southern shooting and another cover-up, only this time it had happened in my own hometown with a member of my immediate family as a major culprit.

With the revelations of *The Uprising of '34*, I began a difficult personal reexamination of my earliest years in the South. Fragments of memory from those days growing up in Honea Path swirled through my head. On the surface, it all seemed so ordinary. I was raised in a former mill superintendent's house almost a stone's throw from Chiquola Mill. My father sold equipment and supplies to cotton mills throughout the South. My mother was a local high school history teacher. Not once was I encouraged to work in the textile industry. In fact, to this day I've never set foot inside Chiquola Mill.

I recalled one detail, however. When I was growing up, an old shotgun stood in the corner of a closet in our home. I was told only that it belonged to my grandfather and it had been involved in some ancient dispute involving a labor union. I remained curious about it for years, but when I asked to know more, the responses from my father were always vague and evasive.

The closest thing I remember to a family discussion of the strike came from my grandmother, Emma, Dan Beacham's widow. I recall sitting on her knee as a young child and being told that in the old days Honea Path had been called "Little Chicago"—a reference to gangster violence—in a headline on the news ticker in New York City's Times Square. My grandmother seemed quite impressed by this. To me, it was just another shoot-em-up tale—it had no connection to my own family. As a young adult, long after my grandmother's death, I sometimes asked about that old story. Nobody seemed to remember.

In retrospect, it's hard to believe one could grow up in the midst of a community that had experienced such tragedy and not be aware of it. The fact is, it's almost impossible to keep a secret at all in a small town like Honea Path. Everybody seems to know everything. Gossip moves with the speed of light from front porch to front porch. Date a girl a few times and you're engaged. Make too many purchases in the town's liquor store and you've got a drinking problem. In my college days, whenever I came home for the weekend, my return was written up in the town newspaper!

It became a continuing cat-and-mouse game to try to sneak into Honea
Path unnoticed. I never succeeded.

Yet, the strike of 1934 was one secret the town kept. The topic was
strictly off-limits when I was growing up. Not a single South Carolina
history book probed the details of the Chiquola uprising. Unfortunately,
my interest in the subject peaked a bit late. My father, mother and nearly
all in the family who lived through the events of 1934 had passed away.
My brother, Dan, namesake of his grandfather, was of little or no help.
He felt, like others, that the story was best left alone. It became clear
early on that if I was to ever learn the truth, I would go this one alone.

I initially approached my research as a journalist seeking facts—just as I
would for any other story. Perhaps my detachment was derived from the
acute embarrassment of discovering I had lived through the middle of a
remarkable event, yet had missed it entirely. As my research progressed,
however, I slowly began to understand why I was so disconnected from
the history of my hometown. Fear had caused the town's workers to
internalize their grief. Their way of coping with the violence had been to
construct a societal cocoon that gave the community an illusion of
normalcy and allowed daily life to proceed. This cultural artifice was an
effective mask for over two generations. I had broken out of the cocoon
when I finally left town for college. Now, in taking a new look at my
hometown, I had the important benefit of time and distance. With this
new perspective, everything changed. Like it or not, this new knowledge
would alter the way I see my family, my family's friends and the people
who wield power in my native South Carolina.

My pursuit of this story began with the filmmakers who researched and
created *The Uprising of '34*. I learned that when they decided in 1990 to
take on the challenge of making a film about the Textile Strike of 1934,
George Stoney and Judith Helfand had no idea that they were about to
toss a huge cultural hand grenade straight down Main Street in Honea
Path.

Even Stoney, a North Carolina native and veteran director of more than forty documentary films, was not prepared for the forces his video camera would unleash on this project. At first, Honea Path was only a minor part of the filmmakers' sweeping agenda to document the historic strike throughout the South. But that would change as stories—powerful stories—started to bubble to the surface.

Helfand, a former student in Stoney's documentary filmmaking class at New York University, felt conspicuous and vulnerable when she first visited Honea Path. "I was a little scared to be there. I felt as if I was doing something wrong...like I was a fugitive. I wound up taking on the fear of the town. Instead of talking about what we were doing in a full voice, I spoke about our work in a whisper. People were frightened to talk about the past...about going up against the powers that be. I can't tell you how difficult it was to find this story."

Because I had once worked in television journalism, it fascinated me that Honea Path's secret was finally revealed in a way that the architects of its original cover-up could have never imagined: a video documentary made for television. Yet, after the truth was exposed in 1995, the whole affair took on another strange twist. South Carolina's intensely pro-business establishment, still heavily influenced by the region's textile industry, tried to suppress the documentary, first by banning it from broadcast on its state-supported television system and then by making it difficult for people to see in public places.

As I observed these events unfold, new questions arose about who controls public information and who decides what becomes recorded history. Why, and how, could a mass killing in a small town be successfully erased, not only from the history books, but from the public consciousness of those people most affected by it? What instrument of fear could be so powerful that parents would be afraid to tell the story to their own children? And why, after sixty years, would the leadership of a state continue to try to keep a lid on an important chapter in its own history?

Not surprisingly, perhaps, the answers to these questions connect directly to what I had already learned from the Orangeburg massacre and South Carolina's music and dance culture. That same tangle of Southern values—honor, tradition, prejudice, and pride—were key ingredients in this complex recipe. Only in this case they were seasoned with an intense class struggle between dissatisfied, powerless textile workers and a tight-knit circle of white industrialists accustomed to ruling with the absolute authority of feudal barons.

After the Southern industrialists won the labor war of 1934, they clamped the lid shut, retreating to the old ways in which appearances mean more than substance, mistakes are rarely acknowledged, and shared values—no mater how unorthodox—are vigorously defended, even to the point of using deadly force.

Chapter 15 — Hard Living: from Farm to Mill Hill

To understand the tragedy of Honea Path and why its implications extend into the twenty-first century, I had to turn the clock back to the years just following the Civil War, when life in the Piedmont region of South Carolina centered around the small family farm and a barter economy. In this hardscrabble era, local transportation was primitive, and commercial activity was extremely limited. Families had virtually no income and few material possessions. Sustenance came from the land. The isolated upstate Piedmont was considered backcountry by the more prosperous coastal region of the state, where most of the large plantations were located.

The Piedmont's yeoman farmers planted wheat and corn, and raised hogs and cattle to feed their families. Life for everyone—men, women and even the youngest children—was dominated by long days of hard, manual labor. The physically demanding agrarian life created strong bonds between neighboring families, who helped each other in times of illness, hardship, and when harvesting crops. The Scotch-Irish farmers of the Piedmont were a proud and independent people who took care of their needs in a self-contained community.

Outside events, however, were about to change the region forever. As the Civil War brought an end to one kind of slavery, it created another for small farm families. In the years after the war, capitalism decimated the barter economy. The merchant class bought and took control of the area's farmland. Slave labor gave way to new economic mechanisms such as sharecropping and crop liens. Family farmers found themselves on a treadmill of debt, forced to plant cash crops such as cotton and tobacco just to feed their families and pay the mounting obligations to the merchants who now owned the land. Life on the family farm got harsher.

Investors saw huge economic opportunity in the Carolina Piedmont and poured investment funds into the region. Railroad construction exploded.

As trains began to crisscross the rural landscape, commercial agriculture grew rapidly. The expanding cotton crop spawned a new money-making opportunity: mills to process raw cotton into finished fabrics.

In the 1880s, new cotton mills opened throughout the Piedmont. Along with the mill construction came company-built towns to house and support the textile workers. Honea Path, a tiny rural community about forty miles from Greenville, got its rail connection when the Columbia and Greenville Railroad was built in 1852. But it would be another half century before a cotton mill came to the town. In 1902, the Chiquola Manufacturing Company—named in honor of a local Indian chief— finally opened a mill in Honea Path. The four-story, red brick plant was surrounded by a village of new homes for its workers.

For the struggling farmers of the Honea Path area, Chiquola offered a way out of the misery and poverty that had dominated farm life in the post-Civil War years. An entire family, including children, could find employment in the mill. For the first time in their lives, many workers moved into housing with indoor plumbing and had easy access to a general store that offered a line of credit to mill employees. Life in the textile industry, under the paternal oversight of the mill owners, looked very sweet to the tenant farmers of Honea Path. Never before had their families known such comfort and security.

My grandfather, Dan Beacham, shared a common background with many of his Piedmont contemporaries. Born in 1877, one of eight children of a Greenville County farming family, he received a limited education in a country schoolhouse while working the crops and helping the family earn a living. Unlike previous generations, however, he had the choice of becoming something other than a farmer. At age seventeen, he gave up working the land and, with an older brother, left for a job in the Anderson Cotton Mill, about twenty miles from Honea Path.

Among my grandfather's personal possessions, I found a torn, faded old newspaper clip from the early 1930s that was published in the *Anderson Independent*. It described, with great fanfare, the arrival of the Beacham brothers in Anderson. To the excited young boys, their first glimpse of a cotton mill was "the biggest thing in the world," the article stated. They enthusiastically named the mill Old Number One. "They gazed in awe at the huge steam plant and marveled at the town's streets, which were covered with a thick coat of cinders. In all their mountain experience they had never plowed into anything that in any way resembled that kind of soil," the newspaper noted.

Dan Beacham embraced mill life with gusto. The local newspaper got so carried away with the young worker's enthusiasm that it suggested his quick ascent might be rooted in some kind of spiritual quest. A "big, raw boned, awkward country lad," gushed the *Independent*, "he rapidly acquired knowledge and skill in learning and wisdom, and there is a sneaking suspicion that he enjoyed some kind of an inside connection with visions and dreams, for in a very short time he was running as many looms as his elders of long experience."

For the next eleven years, Beacham worked in a variety of jobs at several Piedmont area mills, learning the nuts and bolts of spinning and weaving. He mastered the Draper Loom, the first automated weaving machine used in the textile industry. In 1905, at age twenty-eight, he joined the Chiquola Mill in Honea Path as overseer of weaving. Within six years, Dan Beacham was promoted to the top job: superintendent.

Chapter 16 — The Benevolent Dictator

In a town whose social, religious and commercial life was dominated by a single company, my grandfather's success at Chiquola Mill demanded far more than simply knowing how to manage a productive textile plant. The job also called for the political and social skills of a benevolent dictator—a firm ruler who could effectively deal with any circumstance in the worker community that might negatively impact the mill's bottom line. So it was no accident that a year before he was promoted to mill superintendent, Dan Beacham was elected to Honea Path's town council and later to the office of mayor. He would hold public office without opposition for the rest of his life.

Occupying the simultaneous positions of mill boss, mayor, and—among other things—municipal judge, elevated my grandfather to the symbolic status of most powerful man in town. Outgoing and affable, he relished his role and the lifestyle that it brought. He always drove the latest model automobile, took month-long Florida vacations in the winter, and enjoyed regular shipments of moonshine whiskey, which were hidden discreetly for him at predetermined pickup points on his route through town.

"He was pretty well fixed," recalled my aunt, Hazel Beacham, an admiring daughter-in-law who often lived in the mill superintendent's home when the family traveled. "He drove good looking cars, had nice clothes, and dressed very well. He chewed tobacco, but he was neat about it. Granny kept him a nice spittoon wherever he sat. He liked dogs as pets and enjoyed the dog races in Florida. He loved to read his newspaper. He bought a very good radio...would listen to the news with Lowell Thomas every evening. He really liked *Amos and Andy*. He was at church every Sunday and sang in the choir. Mr. Beacham never went to college, but was smart. He'd say the cutest things and would just laugh."

His good cheer ended, however, with even the faintest suggestion that he do household chores. It was Dan's wife, Emma; her sister, Betty; and the hired help who did all the cooking and cared for the family's garden, chickens and backyard cow. "Men that came up in that time didn't do a lot of things that men do today," aunt Hazel whispered to me, as if to pass on a family secret. "Today a lot of men get in the kitchen and help their wives. They help clean house and do laundry. Mr. Beacham didn't do things like that unless it was push come to shove," she said, smiling gently. "He had people doing all those things for him. Yes, sir. That's the way it was."

Chiquola's owners provided the Beacham family with one of the town's finest houses in a neighborhood on the "right side of the tracks"—the line drawn by the railroad that dissected Honea Path and divided the community's more prosperous residential and commercial sections from the cookie-cutter wooden houses in the mill village where the workers lived. The railroad track became a powerful symbol, one that represented both the town's lifeline to the outside world and the very definition of social class within its own ranks. "There's always a class difference. You can't live anywhere without that," insisted my aunt, who died in 1996 at the age of eighty-one.

Through hard work and tenacity, Dan Beacham had crossed the town's class divide and become a mill manager. But he was not a mill owner. Nor was he wealthy. His power was perceived, not real. Like the workers he supervised, he had come from poverty and his roots extended to the farm. And, like any other textile worker in the Piedmont region of the South, his personal prosperity was directly tied to the whims of the owners of the mill.

In truth, my grandfather was just another hired hand working for the Hammett family, owners of the Chiquola Manufacturing Company. He served in his job as superintendent at the pleasure of Lawrence Hammett, the mill's president, and his younger brother, James Hammett, the vice president. Dan Beacham's position demanded absolute loyalty to the company. This was no problem. Throughout his career, he repeatedly demonstrated that he was a hard-core company man.

In the early years, most textile workers felt a fierce loyalty to their employers. The mills, after all, had rescued them from poverty. Attempts to unionize early mill workers mostly failed in the South. The lure of a job—any job—was enough to overcome whatever initial objections the workers might have had to the low pay and dismal workplace conditions.

That feeling of gratitude, however, began to fade in the 1920s. Wages were meager and hours long. Workers making five dollars or less each week toiled twelve-hour days in hot, lint-filled factories. Even worse, most of their hard-earned income evaporated after paying for rent, fuel, food and clothing. There was almost nothing to show for a week's work.

Discontent escalated in the mill villages. Instead of offering better pay and improving conditions, mill owners demanded more from their employees. Workloads escalated. The bosses claimed new technologies justified their demands for higher output at the same wages.

Ironically, the mill workers found a powerful ally in an up-and-coming young politician from Honea Path. He was Olin D. Johnston, a former Piedmont farm boy and Chiquola worker who became a populist member of South Carolina's House of Representatives. Johnston, whose anti-corporate rhetoric delighted his working-class constituents, couldn't have been more different than company loyalist Dan Beacham. The gregarious Johnston embraced the concerns of the local mill workers and used his legislative position to hold committee hearings that suggested strikes by textile workers were "final weapons of defense," and placed blame on mill officials who put "more work on the employees than they can do."

It would, however, take the Great Depression to strip the remaining sheen from mill life. Under intense economic pressure, mill owners tightened the screws even further, demanding longer hours and increased output from fewer workers. Still, there was no more pay. The tactic of having fewer workers operate more mill machinery in the same amount of time became known as the "stretch-out." Stressed-out textile workers grew increasingly angry.

Franklin D. Roosevelt, elected to the presidency in 1933, offered the mill workers genuine hope of relief from the dismal working conditions. With his "New Deal" came the National Industrial Recovery Act, progressive new federal legislation that established a national minimum wage, eliminated unreasonably long shifts, and gave workers the right to join unions that could bargain with the mill owners. Finally, America's textile workers thought they had the tools to stage a rebellion.

In Honea Path, Chiquola Mill's workers listened intently to President Roosevelt's fireside chats on radio. Energized by his message of hope, they wrote the charismatic president with complaints of abuse by mill management and pleas for help. Some exercised their newfound right to join a labor union. By 1934, one in every three Southern mill workers— an estimated 180,000—had joined the United Textile Workers of America. In Honea Path, about half of Chiquola's work force became union members.

As I continued to research the history of my hometown, I quickly found there were very few remaining old-timers who could speak firsthand of mill life in the 1930s. Luckily, however, I found Mack Duncan, who, in 1934, was a seventeen-year-old non-union loom fixer at Chiquola mill. "The Chiquola workers wanted better living conditions and more money," Duncan told me. "They didn't have much of anything…no privileges, no money. The workers felt exploited. These weren't union organizers. These were just people who thought they could get what they wanted through the union."

"Those workers were unrealistic," responded my aunt Hazel, no doubt echoing the argument she'd heard her father-in-law make many times. "It's hard to understand those times unless you lived through them. People were walking the roads looking for work. There were long bread lines. People were coming to our house on Main Street begging for food. They were trying to find a job to earn a few cents. People walked [from

South Carolina] to Florida—where a little boom had started—trying to get work. It was a terrible time. How these people thought that textiles could raise any wages at that point has always been a mystery to me."

It didn't take long, however, for harsh reality to dampen the hopes of the workers. The legislation that granted the mill employees their new right to unionize had a serious loophole: The oversight board that administered the law was not an impartial body, but one controlled by the mill owners. As a result, the law allowed the mill bosses to become more powerful than ever. Not only could they continue stretch-out tactics in the workplace, but now they could skirt the intent of the new law by intimidating or firing employees who openly supported the unions.

Desperate and frustrated, cotton mill workers from New Hampshire to Mississippi united to support the General Textile Strike of 1934. The huge protest began on September 1, Labor Day. Within a week almost half a million workers had walked off the job. One by one, mills throughout Carolina's Piedmont region ceased operations. By the end of the first week, 43,000 South Carolina workers had joined the picket lines, shutting down more than two-thirds of the state's two hundred textile mills.

Dan Beacham was angry. For years he had ruled Chiquola's "mill hill" community as a paternalistic boss. On the issue of unions, however, there could be no give and take. He had to hang tough. His bosses, the mill owners, believed that the core viability of their business was at stake. Their superintendent had to take control of the union threat and stop it cold. He must rule on this matter with an iron fist.

Chiquola's union members were powerless in dictating how the plant was run. My grandfather wasn't about to let that change. As mill boss, he had influence over almost every aspect of his workers' lives. He controlled where the town's residents worked and played, even the churches where they worshipped. If a Chiquola employee had a personal problem, he intervened. If liquor consumption got out of hand, he could use his power as the town judge to dish out fines.

His big stick, however, was mill housing. Row after row of nearly identical wooden frame houses lined the streets of the mill village. Chiquola owned and rented the houses—as well as supplied electricity and heating fuel—to its employees. The compact structures looked so much alike that legend has it that a worker, after getting lost one night in his own neighborhood, put a pair of boots on the roof of his house in order to distinguish it from the others.

During the depression, losing one's job at the mill meant losing one's home. The mill used the threat of eviction as a potent instrument of fear. Dissident workers were summarily fired, and—on very short notice— thrown out of their rented houses. With few other options for a place to live in Honea Path, most workers conformed to the mill's authority out of the simple fear they'd be tossed onto the street if they did otherwise.

"Mr. Beacham wasn't too friendly with the workers in the (Chiquola) plant," recalled Duncan. "I wouldn't walk up and talk to him. He was boss man. What he said controlled everything around the mill…in the mill village…everything. When Mr. Beacham spoke, he was in control."

There was no way Dan Beacham was going to give an inch to a labor union at Chiquola Mill. He would defy the union organization and keep Chiquola running. The message he sent workers was clear: If you strike Chiquola, you're fired...and you're homeless.

This time, however, his threats were ignored. The emboldened workers of Chiquola Mill were fed up and ready to fight back. With the backing of their beloved Franklin D. Roosevelt, they thought that they could win.

Chapter 17 — Bloody Thursday

As the textile strike spread like wildfire to mill towns throughout the South, tensions escalated. Schools closed, businesses ceased operations, public events were canceled. A Piedmont newspaper, the *Spartanburg Herald*, reported that "in one short week industry in the Piedmont has been paralyzed...the flow of money has ceased, merchants find their stores robbed of customers, transportation is ruined and all business is disturbed."

On day six, at 5 a.m., the strike reached Honea Path.

About two-hundred striking Chiquola workers were joined for a rally by a "flying squadron" of another one-hundred-fifty or so workers from the nearby mill town of Belton. Using visiting workers to help shut down a mill was an effective tactic widely employed throughout the South. Once their own mill had been closed, workers organized into flying squadrons to visit neighboring mills in hopes of getting non-union employees to join them.

Chiquola's turn came on a warm Thursday morning. In anticipation of the strike, the mill had hired unskilled local farmers to replace employees who refused to work. Union supporters were furious at the tactic. There was also suspicion that workers from closed mills in nearby towns might be temporarily filling the jobs of Honea Path strikers. Bringing the contingent from Belton offered an added benefit: they could identify any of their own members who might be working undercover at Chiquola.

In the pre-dawn hours, the flying squadron left Belton for the seven-mile ride to Honea Path. Waiting in front of the mill were the locals from Chiquola. Though some were strong union supporters, others were ambivalent about the strike and had only come at the request of co-workers. A few showed up just to see the action. As the crowd gathered, they sang "We Shall Not Be Moved." Overhead, a huge American flag flapped in the humid morning air.

At larger mills throughout South Carolina, pro-union demonstrators were met at the front gate by armed National Guardsmen and scores of local policemen. Chiquola Mill, however, didn't rate such help. In the days prior to the Honea Path protest, Dan Beacham's repeated requests that National Guard troops be sent to protect his mill fell on deaf ears. South Carolina Governor Ibra C. Blackwood, who had called up every available guardsman for strike duty, told Beacham he could not send troops to Honea Path because there had been no previous labor trouble at the mill.

Frustrated, my grandfather emulated the tactics of other small mill operators throughout the region. He created his own security force. Using his power as the town's mayor, one-hundred-twenty-six local men were deputized for mill duty. Most were favored workers. All were anti-union. The new "special officers" were armed with an assortment of pistols, rifles, shotguns, and even a World War I-era machine gun, nicknamed the "water cooler" because it used a water-filled cooling system to dissipate the heat from sustained fire.

As dawn approached on September 6, the mood outside Chiquola was upbeat. The assembled workers formed a picket line across the mill's entrance. Dan Beacham was one of the first to arrive. He was allowed to cross the line. Once inside the mill, he started using the telephone. "I called the president of the union and told him the mill would not start today, but asked that we be allowed to send a man into the building to start the water pumps for the village," he told local newspaper reporters on the scene. Then he made a series of last-ditch calls to the governor and other government officials requesting troops be sent to the mill. His efforts failed.

While my grandfather worked the phone, his armed deputies were taking positions at windows along the upper floors of the four-story mill. On the roof, several men mounted the machine gun, but could not to get it to function properly. Below—near the mill entrance—the strikers roamed about unarmed, mingling with onlookers in the crowd.

Though the mill's management had promised that the plant would not open that day, dozens of non-union workers somehow got past the picket line to enter the building. Others, on the outside, attempted to get in. The strikers were outraged. As dawn approached, the mood turned ugly.

Non-union workers inside the mill began passing wooden "picker sticks" through windows and doors to their supporters on the outside. Picker sticks, used on the mill's looms, are sturdy hickory batons with pointed metal tips. The heavy sticks can effectively double as lethal clubs.

Alarmed by the distribution of these potential weapons, strikers grappled with non-union workers, trying to take possession of the sticks. Random fist fights broke out. Workers on the opposing sides wrestled each other to the ground. Scuffles spread rapidly throughout the crowd.

Then suddenly, without warning, a single shot rang out. Another quickly followed, then another, and another, escalating into a furious hail of bullets and buckshot. The shots crisscrossed the demonstrators, some coming from the mill windows above and others from weapons at ground level. As the panicked workers turned away and tried to flee for their lives, the firing continued. The fusillade lasted about three minutes.

As abruptly as the gunfire had begun, it stopped. There was silence, broken only by the painful groans and sobbing of the wounded men. Lee Crawford and Ira Davis, brothers-in-law, lay mortally wounded in the grass near the entrance to the mill. Claude Cannon—shot five times— bled profusely, and then died, on a sidewalk directly across the street. Maxie Peterson, Bill Knight, and Thomas Yarbrough all lay dead. C. L. Rucker, critically wounded, would die within three days.

Seven workers were killed and thirty wounded on "Bloody Thursday." Had the machine gun mounted on the roof of the mill not malfunctioned, there would have many more.

Chapter 18 — "Cold-blooded Murder"

When the dust settled in Honea Path, investigations determined that not one of the striking workers at Chiquola Mill had been armed. Nearly all of the victims were shot in the back. Most had been wounded while trying to flee the scene.

The union called the shooting "nothing short of plain slaughter." An organizer told reporters: "Union men didn't have a chance. They were shot down like dogs as they fled from an armed mob which attacked them without just cause. The unionists went to the mill on a peaceful mission and [were] unarmed. They were met with a burst of gunfire..."

Mack Duncan, who was in the mill office when the shooting erupted, blamed the mayhem on Chiquola's bosses. "The company did it. They deputized any man that wanted to be a deputy. If he could get a gun, they let him have a gun. There were a lot of guns at the mill that day."

Chiquola's management expressed no remorse for the killings. To the contrary, the company continued its aggressive anti-union stance by promptly banning funerals for the slain workers at any of the mill-owned churches. As it turned out, the churches weren't big enough anyway.

The town of Honea Path, a place few had heard of the week before, was now on the front pages of the nation's newspapers. Passenger trains, Model T automobiles and flatbed trucks brought ten thousand mourners, including labor and religious leaders, from across the nation to attend the funeral for the slain workers. Newsreel cameras documented the event. It was the largest crowd ever to gather in the tiny community.

As the massive funeral began in a grassy field just outside of town, the sea of mourners joined to sing the hymn "In the Sweet Bye and Bye." They faced a row of gray wooden coffins, shaded from the afternoon sun by a brown tent. When a union leader silently raised the bullet-ridden flag carried by strikers two days before, many sensed they were part of a pivotal event in the labor movement's efforts to organize the South. "We are in the midst of our fight for democracy, and will continue to fight until we win," said George L. Googe, southern head of the American Federation of Labor.

Furman Rodgers, another strike leader, called the Chiquola Mill shootings "cold-blooded murder." He predicted my grandfather and Gov. Blackwood would "feel the brand of Cain" for their role in the shooting of the strikers.

Against a backdrop of American flags gently rippling in the breeze, Rev. James Myers said that the textile workers were engaged in "a religious war" and it was "a Christian duty" that all workers support the strikers. "These men need not have died if their employers had realized the right of the workers to organize, the right to which they are entitled as children of God," he said. "They died to make industry Christian."

As the caravan of funeral hearses began the solemn procession toward local cemeteries, several mourners quietly chanted "Remember Honea Path, remember Honea Path." For a brief moment, it looked as if the Honea Path tragedy might very well be recognized as the turning point of one of the largest grassroots movements in American labor history. But remembrance was not what the textile industry had in mind.

Within forty-eight hours after the slain workers were laid to rest, Chiquola re-opened. Within two weeks, the national textile strike collapsed. Exhausted workers ran out of food and money. The union didn't have the resources to sustain the protest. It was a devastating defeat for the textile workers. The strikers ended up with nothing for their efforts. There was no pay raise, no union recognition, not even the guarantee of their old jobs in the mill.

For the workers of Honea Path, there was to be no justice for the massacre. Though a coroner's jury charged eleven men with murder, none was convicted. Legally, the case was quickly closed.

The only official eyewitness accounts of the day came from the ninety-nine people who testified at a two-day coroner's inquest in Honea Path's town hall. From that testimony, the *Anderson Independent* newspaper concluded that every worker who died and most that were wounded "were shot while fleeing with their hands raised, from behind, or while lying helpless on the ground."

During the inquest, Guy Cannon, a union supporter, testified that he witnessed E. T. Kay, a Honea Path police officer, shoot Thomas Yarbrough in the back with a pump shotgun. "Yarbrough had his hands in the air, and was running away when he was shot," Cannon said. O. R. Magaha testified that he witnessed the shooting of Lee Crawford by Rob Calvert, one of the "special officers" deputized for mill duty. "Rob Calvert got his gun out and pointed it at Crawford declaring 'Damn you, I'll kill you.'" Seconds later, Magaha said, Calvert shot Crawford at close range. Another witness, R. W. Jones, said he saw policeman Charles Smith approach the wounded Crawford as he lay bleeding on the ground. "Smith shot him several times while he was down," Jones said.

Two witnesses told the coroner's jury that Dan Beacham was among those firing a weapon during the melee. J. A. Magaha, who said he did not picket at the mill that day, testified that Beacham shot at him from fifty to seventy-five feet away. "Mr. Dan Beacham was at the back door of the mill office shooting at me with a pistol," said Magaha. His testimony was corroborated by Paul Moon, a young union supporter. "Dan Beacham, the mayor of the town and superintendent of the mill, did some shooting," Moon testified.

Though present in the courtroom when the accusations against him were made, my grandfather was never called to testify in the investigation. However, in reaction to allegations at the coroner's inquest, he issued a written statement: "I was surprised to hear some people swear that they saw me shoot at them from the mill office door. The truth is well known to most all of the citizens of Honea Path. It had been decided that to open the mill the morning of September 6 might precipitate a riot and that, therefore, we would not start the mill. I, shortly thereafter, went to my home about a mile away for breakfast and was there when all the shooting and fighting took place. I was so far away I did not even hear the shots, and knew nothing of it until I returned to the mill after it was all over."

Beyond that statement, there was no further public explanation by Dan Beacham of why he would choose to leave the mill to have breakfast in the midst of such a tense situation. However, in 1995—sixty-one years after the shooting—the last remaining survivor among the wounded workers offered his own explanation to me: Dan Beacham lied. He was not at home having breakfast as he said, but was standing beside the mill office during the shooting, William Andrews Smith, then eighty-four, said in an interview for this book.

Smith, twenty-three-years-old and ambivalent about the union in 1934, said he walked past my grandfather, who was with Honea Path police chief George Page and a local law enforcement officer, only seconds before being hit. A bullet passed through his back, just missing his spine. Smith said he had absolutely no doubt that Dan Beacham was there. "He was at the plant office outside just seconds before I was shot," said Smith, who died in early 1999.

My grandfather and the Hammett family, Chiquola's owners, also tried to distance themselves from the provision of weapons to the gunmen at the mill on the morning of September 6. James D. Hammett, Chiquola's vice president, was in the mill that day. In 1995, Hammett, then eighty-six, told reporters from the *Greenville News* that "we had no idea there would be any shooting. The mayor of Honea Path [deputized workers] but he didn't, as far as I know, give any guns out."

That view was disputed by B. F. Hughes, the mill's night watchman in the early morning hours of September 6. According to an unpublished personal memoir by his granddaughter, Kathy Lamb, Hughes told his wife that Dan Beacham came into the mill very early that morning as weapons were being loaded into the building. "Mr. Beacham had come to him and told him to go home and not breathe a word of anything he saw to anyone," Lamb wrote. "If he did, he would lose his job."

Hughes went home as told and was not at the mill during the shooting. But later he was called to testify at the inquest. Tempering his story a bit, Hughes told the jury that he had seen some men with weapons in the mill that morning, though he could not recall most of their names.

"My grandfather told in his testimony the very thing he was told not to tell," wrote Lamb. "He told that he saw the guns brought into the mill but refused to tell the names of the people who did the deed. I guess he thought if he didn't mention the names that it would save him from getting fired. But, he was wrong. He was fired two months after the trial [inquest] and blacklisted from all the mills in the area."

It was only with help from Olin D. Johnston, the former Chiquola worker who had been elected South Carolina's governor in 1934, that Hughes later got a job with the Works Progress Administration. Other workers, even those with the most remote connection to the 1934 strike, weren't so lucky. Most of the strikers were blacklisted. They became victims of a wave of threats, intimidation and harassment by Southern mill operators that would generate fear among textile workers for the next three generations.

Chapter 19 — The Grief of Iona Cannon

I saw Sue Cannon Hill for the first time on television. Her grief-stricken words in *The Uprising of '34* upset me. Teary and emotionally fragile, she told in a gripping interview how the management at the local textile mill—led by my grandfather—had nearly destroyed her family. But when she spoke his name, she put a knife through me. I'd never heard my family name spoken that way. *Beacham.* Contempt dripped from the word. To her, it was the name of a mass murderer, the man who killed her father and destroyed her mother. It was a name she'd never forget...or forgive.

In late 1994, I was planning to return to South Carolina for the Christmas holidays. I wrote a letter to Sue Hill, telling her who I was. I apologized for what my grandfather had done. I told her I had been surprised to learn what happened to her father and mother, and wanted to know more. I asked what I could do to make things right. Would she allow me to visit? Could we talk about it?

A couple of weeks went by before I heard back from her. I later learned that she, like others I had written at the time, saw the name *Beacham* in the return address of my envelope and had been unable to open the letter. Finally, after a few days, their curiosity won out. One of her friends told Sue that my letter to her had been harmless, and it might be okay after all to read what I had sent. A relieved, but hesitant, Sue Hill called and invited me to her home during the Christmas holiday.

As I approached the sprawling modern ranch house where Sue now lived with her husband, I couldn't help but be surprised at how far she had come from the days of living in poverty with her mother on Chiquola's mill hill. Sue had married a prosperous businessman, I was told, and this home—one of the nicest in town—fronted fifty acres of land with two private fish ponds.

I was ushered into a huge, rectangular living room with a panoramic rear view of the extended rural landscape. Sue's greeting was gracious, but I sensed that she was not comfortable. Neither was I. We were both walking on egg shells. As we seated ourselves across from each other on comfortable sofas at one end of the room, the Southern tradition of beginning a visit with small talk seemed terribly inappropriate. I knew Sue wanted to know why I was there, and decided it was best to get to the point right away.

I never knew Dan Beacham and was not there to defend him. He was a mystery to me, I told her, and she probably knew more about him than I did. I was horrified by what he had apparently done, and wanted to learn the truth about him. I wanted her to tell me what she knew—warts and all. I wanted to record it on a tape recorder, I told her, so that I didn't miss a word of her story.

She agreed, I clumsily set up the recorder, and we began what was to be a wrenching afternoon.

After Claude Cannon's death at the mill, Sue's mother, Iona Cannon, found herself with no job, six young children to raise, and an eviction notice ordering her to vacate her mill-owned home. Because Honea Path was a one employer town, there was no option of finding alternative work there. Mrs. Cannon, who had no money to relocate, had a simple choice: either lose her home, or go back to work for the very men responsible for killing her husband.

Even more humiliating, she would be allowed to resume her job at the Chiquola Mill only after she pledged to never again utter the word *union*.

The pain in Sue's face was vivid as she recalled the extraordinary grief her mother had endured and was forced to conceal throughout most of her life. "Can you imagine waking up one day with no husband, no job, and six children staring you in the face? Not knowing where your next meal is coming from. That's what my mom faced."

While at least one of the Chiquola widows placed her children in an orphanage, Sue said her mother chose to keep her family together. First, that meant taking a job at the mill—and the oath of silence that came with it. "They talked to her like they wanted to. They told her to either take the job on their terms or leave."

I asked Sue what it was like at home in those days. Did her mother ever talk about what happened to their father at the mill? No, she responded, Iona Cannon's grief played out not in words, but in actions—sometimes bizarre actions.

One was a morbid habit. At night, Mrs. Cannon often sat quietly for hours at home clenching the blood-soaked clothes her husband wore at the time of his death. She stopped only after Sue's brother, Marvin—who could no longer endure the routine—took his father's tattered garments and buried them in a nearby field.

Even then, Mrs. Cannon refused to let go. She searched the ground near her home, digging in various spots in a fruitless effort to recover the clothes.

Sue's father, Claude, was killed on a sidewalk across the street from the mill's main entrance. After being shot three times in the back and twice in the hand, he bled profusely, leaving an immense blood stain in the concrete. Over time, Sue told me, the stain faded and was barely visible —except when the sidewalk was wet. "When it rained the blood stain would come back a dark, copper-looking color. A lot of people came to look at the 'bleeding sidewalk' when it rained. The neighbors complained, but the mill wouldn't do anything."

Then, about eight years after the shooting, the two sections of stained concrete were quietly removed. Honea Path's legendary "bleeding sidewalk" was suddenly no more.

It didn't matter to Iona Cannon, who, after her husband's killing, never set foot on that sidewalk again. "We had no car and walked everywhere.

Whenever we went into town, mom refused to use that sidewalk," Sue said. "She would take us a back way behind the mill through the weeds and we'd cross the railroad tracks to get into town. Only when I was grown did I understand that she didn't want to walk where daddy was killed."

Even with Iona's mill job, the family faced years of poverty and near starvation. "I saw mom diluting a can of Carnation milk with water to make cornbread to feed six children," Sue said, unable to hold back the tears. "It must have been hard for her knowing we were going hungry."

At this point, Sue began to sob. Crying has always unnerved me. I felt guilt for making her tell this story. Should I leave? No, I thought, I'll just wait. We sat quietly. Time froze. It seemed like hours went by. When Sue recovered, I asked if she felt like going on. Yes, she said. Her mother would want this story told. And it was only because I had apologized for the actions of my grandfather, she said, that she decided to see me at all. No one else from the side of the mill's management had ever expressed remorse. Not in 60 years. She was determined to go on.

Composed for the moment, the story continued. On rare occasions, there was unexpected help. Iona would hear a knock on the front door. When she answered, no one would be there. On the porch, however, she'd find several bags of groceries. Though the family never found out who left the food, Iona suspected it was the man witnesses said shot her husband.

"There had to be some sleepless nights for these people," Sue said. "If there weren't, then they didn't have a conscience. I don't know how these people that did the shooting—for jobs or money or whatever—lived with themselves. They shot people whose kids went to the same school with their kids. They shared the same benches in church with the family members of the ones they killed. They watched as the families of these workers nearly starved, living on beans and fat meat or whatever they could find. I think many of them suffered for it the rest of their lives."

About four years after the Chiquola violence, Tom Stalcup, one of the deputized workers who shot at strikers from a mill window, visited Mrs. Cannon. Stalcup told the widow he was ashamed of his role in the shooting and asked her for forgiveness. "He told her he couldn't live right until he made it right with her," Sue said.

Did Stalcup, I asked, tell Mrs. Cannon who gave the order to fire at the workers? Yes, Sue said, her mother had asked that very question. "Dan Beacham," Stalcup had answered. Not only did Dan Beacham give the order for the men to shoot, Stalcup said, but the mill superintendent told the deputized gunmen to kill every striker they could, no matter who it might be. "Mr. Stalcup seemed to have a lot of trouble with this through the years," Sue said.

Iona Cannon died at age sixty-four, never discussing the events at the mill outside of her own home. "Some days she'd talk about it. Other days she wouldn't. She never got over my father. Never," Sue said. "But I never saw her show any hate...not one word against them."

Chapter 20 — Breaking a Social Contract

The heartbreaking story of Iona Cannon shocked me. It simply could not have happened in the Honea Path I thought I knew. How many others in the community had suffered her same fate? How could such a tragic situation openly play out in a Bible belt town where a majority of the townspeople had worn their Christianity as a badge of honor? Even though things had gone terribly wrong on one very bad morning in 1934, how could its horrible aftermath continue uncorrected for sixty years? Those at the mill who had originally intimidated the workers, after all, were long dead. Why then was the worst tragedy in Honea Path's history still considered a taboo topic, a secret to be denied later generations?

"It wasn't just a secret. It was much bigger than that," Judith Helfand, the documentary producer, surmised. "It was a contract, a social contract about how to survive and live in a town for the next sixty years. If you want to work here, you're going to have to do this. If you want to stay in your house, you're going to do this. This is the deal. If you want to be part of this town's society, this is what you know and this is what you don't know."

She nailed it. There's a knee-jerk denial of unpleasant truth that has long run deep in South Carolina's culture. Many locals in Honea Path, siding with the mill owners, had long ago been convinced that the workers were entirely to blame for their fate at Chiquola. The discussion was closed years ago. This allowed for an easy and convenient rewrite of history that made it acceptable to ignore the pain and poverty of those who didn't buy into the official story. Most of the town had signed on to the social contract. Those who didn't kept their mouths shut. Over time a shell (the cocoon) was built around the community and the shared myth became a historical facade.

It would take a powerful weapon to break that myth and destroy the facade. That weapon, a film, came along in 1995. But, even then, the old fiction would fall hard. As hard as many of the white establishment in

South Carolina, including my own brother, tried to portray *The Uprising of '34* as a work of union propaganda, they failed to challenge its extraordinary scholarship. The project, organized to record the stories of the 1934 strike survivors, was backed by a remarkable collaboration of nearly sixty scholars, educators and community activists. The film had genuine credibility—something the local mythmakers had never really needed before.

Of the many ways the documentary opened my eyes, one involved a very powerful local prejudice held by my parents and their friends. Without exception, they all vehemently detested labor unions. I clearly remember my father's proud, oft-repeated reminder to me that South Carolina is "a right to work state." For years, I didn't know what that meant and didn't really care. Now I understand. "Right to work" means workers do not have to join a union even if that union has a labor agreement with their employer. Another term that applies to South Carolina, "employee at will," means that a worker can be fired by an employer at will, no reason needed.

These strong pro-corporate policies, coupled with the collapse of the labor movement in the 1930s and the continued failure to rebuild it, turned South Carolina into one of the most union-hostile environments in the nation. The state proudly advertised to out-of-state businesses that it had one of the lowest percentages per capita of union membership in the United States. As a result of plentiful cheap labor and generous long-term tax breaks offered by the state government, large corporations such as BMW, Michelin and Fuji opened plants in the Piedmont area in the 1990s.

One unfortunate irony of the late twentieth-century industrialization of South Carolina's Piedmont was that workers actually paid more of their income for the privilege of having access to lower-paying jobs. The state's residents were assessed higher personal and property taxes to subsidize the lucrative state-brokered deals used to attract multinational corporations to the region. They also took on the continuing burden of paying for the added congestion and pollution these industries brought to their neighborhoods.

Due to South Carolina's strong thirst for economic growth, anti-union propaganda from the state's business interests has been carefully crafted through the years. The messages, targeted to lure outside business to the state, have been so successful that a general dislike of organized labor is now tightly woven into South Carolina's culture. The word *union* has been demagogued to a hot-button, dirty-word status by corporate leaders and politicians alike in the state.

It was against this backdrop of a deep cultural hostility toward labor unions that the story of Honea Path came to light. From the beginning, I saw the saga of the Chiquola workers as the recovery of an important piece of misplaced history—not as a story about heroes of organized labor. I believed this cultural find would be welcomed—perhaps not by some families, my own included—but by a grateful community who would finally learn of an essential force that shaped their town for most of the past century.

To my surprise, I was wrong.

Chapter 21 — Going Home Again

In the fall of 1994, I learned of an effort in Honea Path to establish a monument to honor the slain workers at Chiquola Mill. Immediately, the idea struck a chord. Even though a monument is only symbolic, in this case—because of the secrecy surrounding the killings—it would make a powerful statement. Finally, a community would shed years of fear and shame and publicly acknowledge its hidden past. The idea grew on me.

At the same time, I realized, as the grandson of Dan Beacham, my public support of such a project would be controversial, both to my own family and to the families of those whose loved ones were killed. So be it, I thought, a little controversy is exactly what's needed to wake Honea Path from its sixty-year sleep.

My first act was to write letters to people whose compelling interviews I had seen in *The Uprising of '34*. One had been to Sue Cannon Hill. Another was to Kathy Lamb, the gutsy former textile worker who conceived the Workers' Memorial project and, with her husband, Robert, raised the money to build the monument. Kathy had first learned of her own father's involvement in the events at Chiquola during the making of the film, and her new knowledge had sparked a fire. During that same Christmas holiday that I met Sue Hill, I also visited Kathy and Robert for the first time at their home.

We hit it off, all sharing similar responses to the odd circumstances of suddenly confronting our unknown family histories at middle age. Kathy displayed a feisty, can-do quality that had the effect of moving the timid from her path. Robert offered just the kind of support she needed to make things happen in a town resistant to change. Together, the Lambs were the perfect couple to spearhead what was a controversial campaign to build a monument to honor the slain Chiquola workers.

Soon after, I was invited to participate in the dedication ceremony for the monument. It would be held on Memorial Day, 1995, in Dogwood Park, a small tree-shaded area just behind the town's elementary school. For the Lambs, the road to this day was long and hard. Though Honea Path's town council had voted unanimously to approve installation of the monument, the couple had hit roadblocks along the way. Every detail, from raising the money in small contributions to staging the ceremony, had been a tricky obstacle course that required a mix of stubbornness and diplomacy. Mayor Billy Gilmer, one of my high school classmates, warned that honoring the slain workers would revive the old passions that led to the town's collective amnesia. "There were wounded people who weren't killed," Gilmer told the *Greenville News*, "and there were the people who did it and got by with it. All those families are still in town."

One of those who criticized the monument was James D. Hammett, at the time the only living connection to Chiquola's 1934 management. In a newspaper article in the *Greenville News*, Hammett said that his family felt no responsibility for the shootings of the mill workers. "No, I don't think the family felt anything about it," he said. "...[The] people that were killed were union people. I was against the union and I'm sure Lawrence [his brother and president of Chiquola Manufacturing Co.] was." As to the monument itself, Hammett added, "Sixty years later to come up with a monument to them. I think it's absolutely ridiculous."

Because of the strong anti-union sentiment in South Carolina, it would have been very easy for the people of Honea Path to dismiss the workers' tribute as an act of labor propaganda. I didn't want to see that happen. I argued that the story was an important piece of local history that the community had been denied. Whether or not one supported the labor movement didn't matter one bit. The town's citizens should recover their missing history if for no other reason than to better understand themselves.

Having been raised by a mother who was a history teacher, I knew that what's taught as history—at the least the "legitimate" version presented in school textbooks—is often determined by those that hold power. But, to me, the saga of Honea Path's workers in the textile strike was something special. It was the "lost" story of my own hometown, a tragedy that had made a subliminal impact on two generations of local residents. As newly recovered history, it would be preserved and studied for future generations. This was the work of serious scholars, and—I felt with certainty—would be recognized as such.

The last thing I expected, especially in this so-called information age, was a widespread attempt by South Carolina's corporate interests to suppress the Honea Path story. Yet, in early 1995, that's exactly what happened.

In January, Spartanburg Technical College, a school supported with public funds from the state of South Carolina, canceled "Who Builds America," a five-week community-interest course that was to examine the history of working people in the South. One session was to have included a screening and discussion of *The Uprising of '34.*

The instructor of the canceled class was Simon Greer, a graduate student in social history and a part-time employee at the Carolina Alliance for Fair Employment (CAFE), a non-profit workers' advocacy group in nearby Greenville that supported the memorial in Honea Path. After being interrogated by a tech school official about his political views, Greer said he was told after the cancellation that it would be "politically unwise" to present the course because certain textile and automotive industry executives that use the school were upset that he was teaching the workers "how to uprise" in his classes. "They'll make you disappear," the school official told Greer. "We get a lot of money from industry, and they don't want us to teach workers their rights."

Others also had difficulty securing venues for screening the film. An English professor was told by the president of Tri-County Technical College in Pendleton, South Carolina that his previously scheduled screening of *The Uprising of '34* was canceled. A history professor found his screening canceled at the Greensboro Historical Museum in North Carolina. He was told point-blank that the museum received money from the textile industry and "wanted to stay neutral" in the community.

Finding a screening room in Honea Path even proved difficult. Use of the town's middle school was secured only after sponsors circumvented the fearful local school principal and appealed directly to the county school board.

Perhaps most blatant was the refusal of South Carolina Educational Television (SCETV) to broadcast the documentary. Funded by the state's taxpayers to provide educational programming for its citizens, the state network stalled and then refused to broadcast *Uprising* even after it was aired as part of the acclaimed *POV* series on public broadcasting stations throughout the United States. Henry Cauthen, then the autocratic head of SCETV, refused to give a reason for suppressing the program. But it was widely assumed that the state's business establishment was behind the move. And it could not be ignored that Mr. Cauthen's late father was for many years a powerful lobbyist for the textile industry in South Carolina.

So, with the corporate roadblocks in place and little interest from South Carolina's mass media, the effort in 1995 to get the Chiquola story out began on a word-of-mouth, neighbor-to-neighbor basis. Whenever asked, I tried to convince people to put aside old myths and take a fresh look at the events of 1934. I argued that the slain workers were actually heroes who had died in a cause to improve the quality of life for themselves and their families. They did something few of us do any more. They risked everything—their jobs, their freedom and, ultimately, their lives—for a cause they believed in. They made a decision to defend their values and to exert some control over their changing place in an increasingly industrialized world. Their method, like it or not, was to attempt to organize their fellow workers into a labor union.

In several front-porch debates, I defended myself against the notion I was "stirring up trouble" by trying to revive an old controversy that was best left alone. More often than not, I found, people were open to at least hearing more about what had happened in their town sixty years earlier. But, the anti-union sentiments and lingering fear of the old days died hard. Why, I was asked repeatedly, did I have to revisit an event that had caused such pain in the town? Why not just leave this old story alone?

"Because," I responded to one of my former grade school teachers, "I'm curious, and I have a right to know, damn-it. Didn't you encourage me to study history when I was in your class?" She paused, looked at me for a few seconds, and said, "I knew you were a troublemaker back in grade school!"

As the date of the Memorial Day workers' tribute neared, activities were stepped up to spread awareness of the event to as many people as possible. Bypassing the major media gatekeepers in South Carolina, the organizers decided to appeal to the local media—in this case community radio and the weekly newspaper. To accomplish this, however, it was important to overcome the common perception that the memorial was to be nothing more than a union pep rally. With the support of the Lambs and the documentary producers—George Stoney, Judith Helfand and editor Suzanne Rostock—I tried to help generate some constructive publicity for the event.

I started with an old mentor. I had worked from the ninth grade through high school graduation at a local radio station with popular Piedmont radio personality Matt Phillips, who owned WRIX, the key radio station serving Honea Path. He and I shared a mutual love of community broadcasting and had remained friends throughout the years. Matt, however, was a very conservative guy and had been warned of the controversial nature of the Chiquola shootings by his local advertisers. He had no intention of touching this hot potato and firmly let me know I wasn't going to change his mind.

Events, however, soon forced his hand. Rumors began to circulate that a camera crew had been in Honea Path making a movie about the strike. Calls on the subject started trickling into Matt's morning talk show. The town's infamous gossip mill picked up the story. Callers began making outrageous claims about how the Honea Path shootings had become the subject of a major Hollywood film. Matt and his co-host, Bev Brandon, were caught off-guard by their listeners and didn't quite know how to respond.

Sensing opportunity, I called Matt and urged him to at least correct the callers on the air. By not having the facts, I argued, he was only adding fuel to the rumors. He agreed, finally warming up to the idea of addressing the topic on the air. But he didn't want to go it alone. Reluctantly (perhaps *painfully* is the better word), he suggested that I do a brief on-air interview with him to address the rumors and clarify the situation.

We scheduled the live telephone interview for the morning of February 20. I had a dental appointment later that morning, but Matt assured me I wouldn't be late. Our chat would last only a few minutes, he insisted. There was no way he would dwell on the Chiquola shootings. We'd do our bit, and then he would quickly move the show to a safer topic.

I called the radio station at the scheduled time from my New York City apartment. At first, our conversation went just as planned. Matt treaded lightly, walking on eggshells. I was sensitive to his concern, but was determined to use the air-time to get our story out to his local audience. I started by offering a little background on the documentary, explaining why I supported it and why I thought the workers' memorial was a good idea.

Then something extraordinary happened. My brief phone-in interview turned into a two-hour town meeting. Caller after caller queued up to tell a personal or family story relating to the strike. Suddenly, the sixty-year silence had broken. The genie, contained for so many years by the mill owners, was out of the bottle. Nearly everyone was positive to the idea of finally getting the story of Chiquola out into the open. During the entire broadcast, only one caller criticized my efforts.

As the show progressed, Matt went from surprised to relieved to euphoric. More than anything else, he was a seasoned radio performer. He knew instantly he had tapped a deep well of emotion in his audience. About midway into the program, Matt stunned everyone by promising on the air to do a live remote broadcast at the dedication of the workers' memorial. As a highly visible and respected member of the community,

Matt had significant power to sway public opinion. His tacit
endorsement—a miracle in light of his anti-union views—gave the
memorial a new air of legitimacy. This staunchly conservative radio host
put aside his personal feelings and stated publicly that the Chiquola story
was one that area citizens should know. That broadcast, and the
subsequent stream of calls on the subject in the days ahead, was—in my
opinion—the turning point in gaining broad public support for the
workers' memorial in Honea Path.

Though radio can be a powerful unifying force in a small town, I felt it
was also important to create a simple written document that explained
why I supported a public memorial that honored the Honea Path Seven
and to give the community a clear explanation of what these men died
for in 1934. I called Elaine Ellison-Rider, editor of the local newspaper,
and asked her if I could write an op-ed article on the subject for her
publication. She readily agreed and gave the article prominent display in
the *Belton-Honea Path Chronicle*.

Chapter 22 — "They Died for the Rights of the Working Man"

When Memorial Day, 1995, finally arrived the tension in the air was almost as thick as the stifling humidity. The prospect of rain eventually gave way to muggy, sweltering heat. By mid-afternoon several hundred people had converged in Dogwood Park. It was a diverse group, ranging from curious local mill workers and onlookers to professional historians and students of organized labor who couldn't resist the remarkable event unfolding in Honea Path.

South Carolina's establishment press, having long ignored the story, was suddenly interested. Video camera crews and photographers circulated through the crowd. Matt Phillips parked the WRIX remote truck on the nearest roadway and began his live radio broadcast. The management of Chiquola Mill, owned at the time by Springs Industries and no longer under Hammett family control, donated food to the event.

Family members of the slain workers—there were fifty relatives of Claude Cannon alone—sat together under large tents provided by a local funeral home.

The ceremony began with a welcome from the town's mayor, Billy Gilmer, who had been a student in my mother's history class. Although he had taken heat from some Honea Path residents over his support of the memorial, Gilmer eventually warmed to the idea of honoring the workers when he made some discoveries about his own family history.

"I had an uncle inside the mill. I had an uncle outside the mill that was shot," Gilmer said, surprising the gathering with his personal finding. "That's the reason it's not talked about today. It was family-to-family, neighbor-to-neighbor. With this dedication, let this be a time of healing for the community."

Then came Sol Stetin, an old-style labor leader who once served as president of the Textile Workers Union of America. At age eighty-five, the fiery veteran organizer raised the passion level of the event. "The men we honor today did not die in vain," Stetin barked with evangelistic fervor. "They sacrificed for those who followed them. We honor them best by making sure that our generation protects what they built."

Moments before I walked to the microphone to publicly acknowledge the role of my grandfather in the tragedy, I was distracted by a chilling image. On a nearby hill, my brother, Dan, stood cross-armed next to the town's police chief. Behind them were several uniformed highway patrolmen and a pair of unmarked state police cars. They all watched silently, just as I suspected my grandfather and his armed deputies had done in the minutes before the shooting six decades earlier.

The brief flicker of fear that seized me at that moment was the first uneasiness I'd felt during the entire day. It was not that I ever thought there would be any violence in the park that day, it's just that I knew too well how things play out in South Carolina. If there's going to be any trouble here, I thought, it will somehow come because of this presumptuous show of armed force. It always has.

I wasn't the only one who felt edgy. Kathy Lamb remembered standing near Sue Cannon Hill when one of the balloons that decorated the park accidentally burst. Both instinctively ducked, fearing a gunshot. Realizing their shared, but unspoken fear, they exchanged glances and began to laugh hysterically.

After the speeches, the ceremony ended with the unveiling of a two-thousand pound burgundy granite monument that named and honored the seven workers shot and killed at Chiquola Mill. The inscription included shooting victim Maxie Peterson's last words: "They died for the rights of the working man."

It was a liberating moment. Not only did the monument honor the dead for the first time, but it signaled an end to the crippling silence that had haunted the town's residents for so long. There was nothing to be afraid of anymore. No one was going to lose their job. No one was going to be evicted from their home. There would no longer be any repercussions for openly talking about unions or what happened at the mill in 1934.

It also gave permission to a younger generation—previously unaware of the shootings—to question and share memories with family members old enough to recall what happened in 1934. In the days that followed, inquisitive children used tape recorders to interview their once-fearful grandparents about Chiquola. For the first time, the tragedy became a topic in school classrooms. Middle-aged adults, like myself, compared notes, trying to identify the subtle ways the shootings had affected our years growing up in Honea Path.

Chapter 23 — Postscript

My grandfather's health declined after the shooting and he soon left his job at the mill. In his final days, his big Buick was chauffeured around Honea Path by a black man who had once worked at Chiquola. In 1936—only two years after the Chiquola massacre—Dan Beacham died of heart failure.

After a period of interim management, Rob Calvert, a Chiquola worker acquitted of murder in 1934 despite the incriminating testimony of thirty-six eyewitnesses, became superintendent of the Chiquola Manufacturing Company and the mayor of Honea Path. He served in the town hall until 1950.

"Rob Calvert was very anti-union...a pro-company man, if you know what I mean," said Mack Duncan. "He wasn't scared of nothing. He was a bully-type man. They promoted him after the shooting. People were afraid of him."

If people thought Calvert was a bully, how is it that he and other mill superintendents were never voted out of public office? The answer lies in the old song lyric "don't bite the hand that feeds you," said veteran politician Fred Moore, who served for twenty-nine years as Honea Path's representative in the state legislature and published the town newspaper from 1945 to 1981.

"Living in houses that cost twenty-five cents a room—a dollar for a four-room house—broke on Friday nights, nowhere to go, nothing to do, you're dependent on these people," said Moore, who died in 2001. "That's why you vote for them."

James D. Hammett Jr., Chiquola's vice president and assistant treasurer, died at age ninety-one on June 5, 2000. Although a member of the Historical Society of Greenville, he repeatedly refused to discuss the history of Chiquola Mill for this book. In his obituary, Hammett was described as "a true Southern gentleman."

In early 1996, I joined a diverse group of teachers, lawyers, unions, and community organizations to raise money from independent contributions to purchase air time on a Piedmont commercial television station to broadcast *The Uprising of '34*. All involved in this project felt it was important not to let South Carolina's public television network succeed with the censorship of a historically important story.

Two years later, Henry Cauthen, the head of the state's public TV system and son of the textile lobbyist, was forced out of his job. On June 2, 1998—in the first major public act of Cauthen's successor—*The Uprising of '34* was finally broadcast to the citizens of South Carolina over the statewide television network.

The initial censorship of the *Uprising* documentary highlighted the state television system's longtime timidity when it came to broadcasting stories sensitive to contributors and corporate interests. "When television channels are run by government agencies, they tend to become a mouthpiece for the interests of that agency," said *Uprising's* co-producer George Stoney. "It was some people's suspicion that this might reflect badly on their inheritance. And they didn't want to offend anybody."

In 2001, while reminiscing about the events at Honea Path during a breakfast in New York, Stoney's producing partner, Judith Helfand, told me a story she'd never mentioned during our many public appearances together. It was how this self-described "Jewish girl from New York" persuaded some of the reluctant textile workers to open up to her and tell their personal stories on camera.

"I was doing a balancing act in Honea Path," she recalled. "It wasn't cool for me to talk about unions there. There's a horrible myth about people like me...Jewish New Yorkers in the South. It's always a group of Jewish New Yorkers who come down and try to get everybody to join a union. Who push people to take incredible personal and economic risks...and then leave. And here I am trying to organize everyone to be in a movie...about unions!'"

The ice was broken one day during a break in an interview with an elderly, ailing worker who was suffering from brown lung disease he had acquired after inhaling cotton fibers for fifty years in a Southern textile mill. Helfand was treading gently, showing the man, who breathed with the aid of an oxygen tank, artifacts from the textile strike. "At one point he leaned over to me while they were changing video tape and whispered, 'Honey, you seem like such a nice girl. When are you going to get a boyfriend, settle down and have a baby?'"

The man hit a nerve. What he didn't know is that just before starting her work on *Uprising*, Helfand had undergone a radical hysterectomy due to cervical cancer. The cancer was a result of her mother's use of the prescription drug DES during her pregnancy. DES—for synthetic estrogen diethylstilbestrol—was prescribed to millions of women between 1939 and 1971 to prevent miscarriages, even though the pharmaceutical industry had known for more than thirty years that the drug was ineffective, carcinogenic, and caused birth defects in lab animals. DES was manufactured and sold by about 250 drug companies throughout the world. It was pulled from the pregnancy market only after young women like Helfand had been diagnosed with rare vaginal cancer.

"I could have told him I'd get around to a baby one day and then have a lump in my throat the rest of the day and be sick, or I could tell him the truth. His question provoked me. I told him I'm not going to have a baby and why."

The old man, stunned, took another deep breath of oxygen. "They kept it on the market anyway! Why would a company do that?"

Suddenly, the elderly Southerner and the young New Yorker connected. "When he asked 'How can a company do that?' I realized that what he really meant was 'How could a company do that to *me*—an educated, middle class Jewish white girl from New York. Because he knew how a company could do that. The mill was directly across the street from his house and cast a shadow in his living room. They did it to him. But he never believed that people like me are ever hurt by companies...it's people like me that own and run these companies. Yet here I was, like him...somebody who had been run over by a company. After that, everything changed. It was one of the most radical moments of my life."

The wall of formality between the interviewer and her subject quickly dissipated. When the camera rolled again, the man's answers were directed to Helfand, with whom he had a newfound empathy. "It did a lot for me, because I was feeling uncomfortable," Helfand continued. "This time, when I asked him about loss, he knew I had lost something just as he had. He spoke differently and I listened differently. We had crossed a divide, and we both knew instinctively that his brown lung disease was connected to my plight as a DES daughter."

As Helfand proceeded with her interviews across the South, she told her personal story only to those that asked. It changed the way she viewed the documentary project, and added a new dimension to the way she felt about issues such as public health, safety, consumerism and workers' rights.

"I believe that people have a right to seek a better quality of life," she continued. "We don't live in a dictatorship. We are not serfs. We have rights as workers to take care of ourselves. I believe that. But it's one thing to believe that, another to know it and live it in your gut, and another to be a student of history and a documentary filmmaker. Up until that point, when my injuries were linked to the injuries of that textile worker, it had all had been very intellectual.

"I found myself listening to retired textile workers telling really, really painful stories about the core choices, or lack of choices, in their lives. Did I have the right to elicit—and ask people to take major-league risks—because they were going to talk about class and break their social contract? You wonder. Are they doing it for themselves? Are they doing it for their grandchildren? Are they doing it to set the record straight?

Who are they doing it for? And what are you going to do for them afterward? What will we do with this footage and this movie? These are huge questions you have to ask yourself. Is this some intellectual exercise, or is my heart in the right place? Am I worthy to listen to these stories of pain, pride and deep, deep ambivalence?"

George Stoney, age eight-six, affectionately described by Helfand as a "leftie white Southern New Dealer," also experienced an unexpected connection during the making of *Uprising* that dated back to his childhood days in Winston-Salem, North Carolina.

"Working on the film made me realize my own terrible class bias," Stoney recalled. "I was reared by an Anglo-Irish fellow—an Episcopalian—who let it be known that I was not to talk to the people who lived next door. They were *those kind of people*...hillbillies and the like. I was in my late twenties before I could hear country music because that was not the kind of music I was supposed to admire.

"I also realized that I physically represented the kind of person many of the people in the South had every reason to hate. That's why Judy and I made such a good pair. She had a big, bright smile. I reminded them of an old foreman that used to be mean to them, or the shoe salesman downtown who insulted them fifty years ago. Making the film made me much more conscious of class feelings. I realized it was far more than just unions. It was class antagonism, which I think still haunts a good part of the South.

"I'm also more understanding of the position of the mill owners in those days," Stoney continued. "It's quite clear that most of them weren't very well off. It was all a very precarious situation. It was a hell of an industry to be in and it was very competitive. Instead of having land agents (as in the sharecropping days), they had their foremen. These foremen decided who worked and who didn't. It was inherently corrupting and bound to collapse anyway. It wasn't an individual venality. I look at the mill owners as the captives of their class and situation."

For me, however, this is a story without end. Each time I return home for a visit, the conversation inevitably turns to the events of 1934. In virtually every situation, there are those who think I'm a troublemaker bent on stirring up painful memories from the past. Others, usually younger people, are fascinated by the whole episode and want to know more.

Some are more passionate than others. During a visit to Honea Path over the Christmas holiday in 1996, my family's long-time physician confronted me in a very public way at lunch hour in a local restaurant. He proclaimed loudly that I should be shot for what I'd done. No jury, he shouted to the gathered diners, would convict the shooter. He wasn't kidding.

Knocking down the facades that obscure the past comes with a price. I've realized I'll never again be able to see my hometown as I did when I grew up there. In a simple and carefree childhood, I had been spared the turbulences of the racial and class divisions inflicted on others who lived less than a mile away. Now, with new knowledge, I see Honea Path as a classic Southern textile mill town—a place precisely designed to divide the homes of mill workers and management, merchant and worker classes, and black and white. I recognize the railroad track that split the town was as much a divide for people as a link for transportation. With my new knowledge, I've gained respect for some townspeople while losing it for others.

Most disturbing of all is that, despite recent efforts, remnants of the old mill hill feudalism remain. With all that's happened since 1995, some textile workers and their families in the town are still afraid to talk publicly about the Chiquola killings for fear they will lose their jobs. Or, due to the residual propaganda of the old mill owners, they continue to feel ashamed about what happened in 1934.

Of course, those who caused the fear are now powerless, and the shame —never justified—was simply part of the myth. Although the workers' efforts ended in defeat and much suffering followed, the deaths of the

Honea Path Seven were not in vain. The disillusionment of the workers and the outrageous conduct by the mill owners made a strong impression on the Roosevelt administration. This helped spur passage of the Wagner Act in 1935 and the Fair Labor Standards Act in 1938. Out of these laws came reforms that vastly improved the lives of all workers, even in states where unionization didn't take hold.

One example was child labor. Before 1938, when the Fair Labor Standards Act outlawed employment of children under sixteen, the practice of "helping" was encouraged by mill managers. Very young children were taught factory skills by their parents and soon "helped" by working in the mill to increase the family's piecemeal earnings. Helping became a form of apprenticeship and a major part of the mill's labor system. Because this practice is now illegal, children have a better chance at a quality life by staying in school rather than being exploited as cheap labor. Other major reforms that came out of the labor unrest were the establishment of the minimum wage and the forty-hour work week.

Whether or not one supports the efforts of organized labor today is irrelevant. Every modern day textile worker—union member or not—has a better quality of life now because of the mill workers who died in Honea Path. Let their story be told, without the ignorance, intolerance and corporate greed that has so long shackled the significant history of the South.

Dan Beacham, mayor of Honea Path and
superintendent of Chiquola Manufacturing
Company, in a portrait from the early 1930s.

The funeral of the slain Chiquola workers drew over
10,000 people to the tiny town of Honea Path.

Acknowledgements

The joy of writing this book was discovering my own story through the stories of others. This volume is the end result of hundreds of brief encounters, conversations and interviews over a period of more than ten years. One of the marvels of the story-building process is how seemingly unconnected fragments of information grow and take form. One day, when you least expect it, comes an "ah-hah" moment. The unconnected connects. The loose pieces come together. At this moment, the real story is born.

This is exactly what happened with the account of Charlie's Place. The seed for the project was planted during a set break for the band at a New Year's Eve party in a hotel in Greenville, South Carolina. As no more than an old college-days fan, I casually approached one of the members of the Tams, a popular Carolina "beach music" group playing that night. I was invited to meet the other band members in their makeshift dressing room. This led to a second visit a few days later in Atlanta, the home base of the band. As I discovered quickly, the Tams were as much fun offstage as on. I was regaled with tales of the road—getting an earful about deadbeat nightclub owners, swindled song writers, and a culinary guide to who makes the best fried chicken in the South.

That day with the Tams steered me to a reunion with my old boss at WCOS, the Columbia radio station where I worked during my college years. Woody Windham, known to his radio listeners as "Woody with the Goodies," is one of those people who could easily challenge Dick Clark as a music-loving "teenager" who never grew up. I told Woody I was interested in writing something about Carolina beach music and its companion dance, the shag. Woody gave me a list of names that would set me on my journey to Charlie's Place. I thank him for his help.

I "discovered" the story of Charlie Fitzgerald's nightclub only after hearing Charlie's name repeatedly mentioned in recorded interviews by old-timers credited with inventing what was to become South Carolina's official state dance. Long talks with legendary Shag Hall of Fame dancers Harry Driver and "Big George" Lineberry opened my eyes to the remarkable creative collaboration that had occurred between blacks and whites in Charlie's long-forgotten club.

In addition to Driver and Lineberry, both now deceased, I want to thank the pioneering dancers who told me their personal stories: Billy Jeffers, Leon Williams, Clarice Reavis, Jean Ferguson, Chick Hedrick, Betty Kirkpatrick, Jo-Jo Putnam and Chicken Hicks.

Also thanks to Lance Benishek, William Holliday, Phil Sawyer, Gene Laughter, Harold Bessent, Norfleet Jones, Hoyt Bellamy, Bo Bryan, Sam McCuen, Miles Richards, Ed Riley, Charles Joiner, W. Horace Carter, Randall Mullins, Jerry Peeler, Leighton Grantham, Jeff Roberts and Paul Robeson, Jr.

Some important musicians, disc jockeys and music industry executives contributed to this book. Thanks to: Bill Pinkney, Jerry Wexler, Jerry Butler, General Norman Johnson, Maurice Williams, Marion Carter, Hoss Allen, John Hook, Eddie Weiss, Ray Whitley, Bill Lowery, Willis and Linda Blume, Charles Pope, Robert Smith, Jackie Gore, Jimbo Doares, Gary Barker, Barry Duke and John McElrath.

And a special thanks to those who were friends and acquaintances of Charlie Fitzgerald: Henry "Pork Chop" Hemingway, Jr., Leroy Brunson, Dino Thompson, Elijah and Dora Lee Goings and Jerome Thomas. They were there and their recollections were essential to preserving an important piece of Southern musical history. I'd also like to express my appreciation to veteran Myrtle Beach photographer Jack Thompson, who graciously searched his files to help locate the only available photograph of Charlie Fitzgerald.

Thanks also to Marc Smirnoff and the staff of the *Oxford American*, the fine magazine of Southern writing in Oxford, Mississippi that published an early excerpt from "Charlie's Place."

It was in the unforgettable summer of 1968, at the Democratic National Convention in Chicago, that I was introduced to journalist Jack Bass. Two years later, he and fellow reporter Jack Nelson would publish *The Orangeburg Massacre*, a groundbreaking book of investigative journalism. (Second edition, ©1984, Mercer University Press ISBN 0-86554-120-5) Without the support of the two Jacks, the pages on Orangeburg in this book simply would not exist.

Also essential to the Orangeburg story was Jim Covington. As chief photographer at WIS-TV in Columbia, Covington used his influence to get the reluctant station management to send a young student reporter to Chicago with him in the summer of 1968. In later years, after he retired, Jim Covington provided essential support for this book by supplying news sources, photographs and a million opinions about what happened at Orangeburg. On one surreal day, he even convinced former governor McNair to meet the author for an "off-the-record" discussion. How he did it remains a mystery to this day.

For their help on the Orangeburg story, I also want to thank Cleveland Sellers, Rhett Jackson, Ramsey Clark, Chad Quaintance, John West, Jordan Simmons, Gladys Simmons, Cecil Williams, Harriet Keyserling, Tom Johnson, Herb Hartsook, Miles Richards, Sandra Birnhak, Bill Hine, Marvin Dulaney, Fred Moore, and Russ McKinney. For their documentary photographs of the people and events associated with Orangeburg, I'd like to thank Bill Barley, Dean Livingston and Jim Covington.

And my appreciation to editor Warner Montgomery and his *Columbia Star* newspaper for publishing early excerpts from my writings on the legacy of the Orangeburg Massacre.

Essential to my discovery of the Honea Path story were New York City-based filmmakers George Stoney, Judith Helfand and Suzanne Rostock. It was their documentary film, *The Uprising of '34*, that first opened the eyes of many Southerners, including myself, to how the General Textile

Strike of 1934 had impacted our lives. Their encouragement, support and friendship were most appreciated.

Special thanks to Kathy and Robert Lamb. Their vision and tenacity led to the creation of the Honea Path Workers' Memorial described in this book. And their unending curiosity and passion made the lost history of Honea Path come alive for a generation who might never have known it.

For the others who helped me navigate this difficult personal story, I'm grateful. They include Tom Terrill, Janet Irons, Keir Jorgensen, Sue Cannon Hill, Bertha Callahan, William Andrews Smith, Mack Duncan, Hazel Beacham, Ellaine Ellison-Rider, Matt Phillips, Bev Brandon, Billy Gilmer, Fred Moore, Tom Langston and Simon Greer.

Finally, I'd like to thank Hettie Jones, the Beat Generation master of poetry and the personal memoir. As the best writing teacher I've ever encountered, her influence on the style of this book cannot be underestimated. My appreciation also goes to Michael Grotticelli, a talented editor with a sense of humor who can be counted on to find that one last mistake that everyone else missed.

My appreciation to all. I only wish the pursuit of history had been this interesting while we were still in school!

Printed in the United States
752300001B

9 781591 131878